P9-CBQ-159

COMPANION

WATCHES

Dean Judy

©2008 Krause Publications

Published by

krause publications
An Imprint of F+W Publications

700 East State Street • Iola, WI 54990-0001
715-445-2214 • 888-457-2873
www.krausebooks.com

Our toll-free number to place an order or obtain
a free catalog is (800) 258-0929.

Library of Congress Control Number: 2007942606

ISBN-13: 978-089689-638-3
ISBN-10: 0-89689-638-2

Designed by Kay Sanders
Edited by Kristine Manty

Printed in China

Contents

Foreword

Buying Time: Collecting Wristwatches

By Reyne Haines

Reyne Haines, owner of Reyne Gallery in Cincinnati, is a regular appraiser on PBS' "Antiques Roadshow." She is the author of *The Art of Glass: The Collection from the Dayton Art Institute* and has contributed to numerous books and articles on collecting.

Haines is also the co-owner and founder of JustGlass.com. She may be reached at 513-504-8159.

The evolution of the timepiece has come a long way over the last few hundred years. Prior to the wristwatch we know today, there were clocks, pocket watches and watches set into bracelets and rings.

Patek Philippe created the first known wristwatch in 1868 for the Countess Koscowicz of Hungary. The band was a thin strap of gold. The dial was white with black enameled numerals, centered in a rectangular case of gold. The dial was hidden by a hinged ornate cover. On the sides of the case were diamonds and enamel, along with flowing swags of gold.

In the early years, wristwatches, also called "wristlets," were thought to be feminine; something to be worn by a lady. Men were only interested in carrying pocket watches. It had been said that a man would "rather wear a skirt than a wristwatch."

The market for men's wristwatches changed when soldiers began wearing them during combat. Pocket watches were cumbersome and made it difficult for the soldier to quickly check the time. By the First World War, wristwatches were in high demand by soldiers. Vintage military watches are highly coveted by collectors today.

As the years passed, there were many more changes to the standard wristwatch. It became more than something that told time. With more complex movements came alarms, day and date of the week information, water resistance and some even offered the phases of the moon. What once was something you had to manually wind would eventually become self-winding, electric, quartz and also LCD.

Watches were also designed to be fashionable. For example, leather or stainless steel bands were suitable for casual attire; solid gold or platinum for formal attire. Plastic bands and cases were also available for the sports fanatic.

Certain manufacturers would eventually be recognized for important world events. Omega was appointed the official time keeper of the Olympic Games and its "Speedmaster" watch was worn by Neil Armstrong as he walked on the moon.

Over time, wristwatches not only became a power statement in the boardroom, they also became collectible.

Collecting wristwatches has become quite the phenomenon, and it's not just for the wealthy. Because of the volume of watches produced over the years, there is something to fit any collector's pocketbook. Early manual-wind, gold-filled Hamilton wristwatches can sell for as little as $50. If you're a big spender, you can take your pick of rarities at the three major auction houses that often fetch over a million dollars.

Some enthusiasts collect brands, some only collect certain eras. There are chronograph collectors, porcelain-dial lovers, mystery-dial addicts and so on.

No matter what your budget, there are a few things you need to keep in mind when collecting. First and foremost, buy only what you like. If you like something, you can never go wrong. Buying something because your favorite celebrity wears one, or because it's the hot new watch of the season, will not necessarily make it increase in value next week, or next year.

Secondly, this book offers a price guide to give you a range in which a watch should sell. Alas, these prices are not set in stone. In some areas, you might find watches selling for considerably more, or considerably less. Supply and demand is what truly creates value, and much like the stock market, what goes up can sometimes go down, too.

A very important thing to consider when collecting watches (or anything) is condition. Condition plays a large role in what any collectible is worth. With that said, there are many aspects to consider when determining condition.

One of the first things you want to know is, "Does it work?" If it doesn't, and you aren't a watchmaker, you might want to rethink purchasing it. If it's a quartz watch, it might just be the battery. If it's self-winding or manual wind, it

Patek Philippe, circa 1955, 18k yellow gold, **$4,200.**

Thanks

Thank you to the following who contributed new photos and other valuable information to this edition: Reyne Haines, Cleves & Lonnemann Jewelers, Tom Harris Auction Center and Hake's Americana & Collectibles Auction.

Thank you also to those who shared their watch-collecting experience, helped with research and allowed their watches to be photographed: Eric Iskin, Bill Hegner, Rene Rondeau, Mary Huff of the American Watchmakers-Clockmakers Institute, National Association of Watch and Clock Collectors members George Roberts, Doyle Cogburn, Fred and Lisa Cooper, Kurt Rothner, Don Levison, Gregg Esses, Armand Gandara, Lance Thomas, Don Allen, Mark Smith, Paul Yu, Brad Johnson, Jim Griggs, Harry Butler, and Bill White; and Swiss watch companies Blancpain, Jaeger-LeCoultre, Longines, Mido, Movado, Ulysse Nardin, Omega, Rado and Tissot.

A thank you also goes to the other generous people who have provided valuable assistance: Anni Wernicke, Chris and Valerie Fain, Dan Nielsen, Troy Garcia, Tom Torgersen, Ned Hassan, Lowell Fronek, and Lisa Jones and Myriam Djela of Antiquorum in New York.

might only need a basic cleaning. Then again, it could be something much more complicated. Finding someone in your area that works on vintage watches can sometimes be challenging. Rarely do today's jewelry stores offer a watchmaker in the back who has the know-how, or even the parts, to repair something vintage.

Another thing you want to consider is the condition of the dial. Remember, watches were made to be worn. They were rarely bought and put away for safekeeping. Some show signs of fading (enameled dials), are missing bar markers or numerals, or have a second hand that has come loose, or perhaps they got wet (and they weren't waterproof). All of these conditions can be remedied, but again, by a seasoned watch specialist.

What if someone has already taken the liberty of having a watch restored before selling it to you? As long as you know what you are buying upfront, and you pay accordingly, all is good. Certain collectors do not want items in their collection that are not in all original condition. That means no replacement hands, no touched-up luminescent bar markers, replaced dials, etc. Restoration may enhance the beauty of a watch, but it can also depreciate the value at the same time. If the watch is common and has condition issues, you should wait until you find one in original condition. With watches that are considered rare, you might be more open to buying one with problems, since finding another example, or one in pristine condition, might be difficult.

On a final note: What was once thought to be a "feminine" item is not often coveted by today's woman. Collecting wristwatches has been more a man's hobby, with women's wristwatches often overlooked. Women frequently view watches as an accessory, or another piece of jewelry; not as a collectible. Perhaps this untapped market is one to watch.

Introduction

Welcome to the fascinating world of vintage watch collecting. The search for, and collecting of, these miniature jeweled time machines is a wondrous journey full of fun, excitement, discovery, profit and knowledge. In this companion guide you will find a great cross-section of pocket watches and wristwatches from the 1870s to today.

What is a vintage watch? Generally speaking, anything made before 1960 is considered to be "vintage." Anything made before 1920 is considered to be "antique." I, however, don't subscribe to any strict lines of distinction and have chosen the arbitrary cutoff date to a "vintage" watch, as any watch that was made before the advent of the LCD (liquid crystal diode) quartz battery-powered timepiece.

The quartz watch started taking over the market in the 1970s, but there are still some extremely col-

After the 1970s, quartz watches ruled the market and still represent the vast majority of timepieces produced today. Bulova Accutron quartz wristwatch with date, **$150-$180**.

lectible mechanical (wind-up) watches to be found from this decade. Quartz watches ruled the market after the '70s and still represent the vast majority of timepieces being produced today. The quartz watch, highly marketed early on by Texas Instruments and Seiko, nearly drove the Swiss watch industry to its knees, and took away the huge market share it had enjoyed for decades. Interestingly enough, it was the Swiss who invented the quartz technology, but at first they ignored it. Fortunately they regrouped, joined in and saved themselves by coming out with watches like the "Swatch Watch." Today, the finest and most valuable watches are still produced in Switzerland and are mechanical (manual wind and automatic wind) timepieces, not quartz.

The later half of the 1800s and early part of the 1900s were high times for watch manufacturing, especially in America, and I consider watches from this period as vintage also. To me a "vintage" watch is one that can be worn and enjoyed, even if it is only on some special occasion. On the other hand, an "antique" watch is one I consider to be so fragile and old, it must remain at rest in a display case somewhere. The 100 years from the 1870s to the 1970s, the period of watch collecting that I love the best, took us from the "turnip" (large rounded pocket watch) to high-tech space-age marvels worn on the wrist.

There could be a hidden treasure in this pile of old wristwatches.

For those of you just starting out in search of a vintage watch, I do hope this book will provide a spark that ignites a passion inside you to study, learn and appreciate the wonderful world of horology, the study of the art and science of time, timekeeping and timekeepers. For those seasoned watch lovers who are reading this, I do hope you find a helpful tip or two inside these pages that may open up other avenues to your searching, and add to the pleasure of discovering just one more beautiful miniature machine.

In search of the vintage watch

There are many ways to search for vintage timepieces and I have had luck with the following:

Classified ads

Focusing your search can weed out the unwanted clunkers and cheaper "throw away" watches that come your way. In general, senior citizens have the lion's share of the vintage and antique watches that lie buried somewhere deep in an old sock drawer long forgotten. I run a continuous want ad in a small local "Senior News" paper that comes out monthly. The secret is to keep the ad running month after month and, as people come across their old watches, your ad will come to mind when they decide to part with them. Your ad might run like this: Watch collector seeks older mechanical (wind up) watches, working or not. Hamilton, Omega, Longines, Rolex, others. No Timex or Quartz. Please contact Bill Smith at 777-222-3333.

I have purchased many fine old timepieces from running ads like this one. I do, however, recommend that you get as much information over the phone as you can. When someone first calls, take the time to ask them a few important questions. Ask if their watch is a wind-up type watch, if that is what you're looking for. Ask if they can tell you what the brand or maker of the watch is. Are they all men's watches? Ladies' watches? Can they tell you approximately how old the pieces are? Can

Benrus BB14 wristwatch, **$40-$50.**

they describe the overall condition to you as average, fine or near mint? If you feel you have a good rapport with the caller, you might find out how much they are asking for the watch, so you can bring the appropriate amount of cash with you. What you are trying to establish by asking these questions is if you are going on a wild-goose chase or have a legitimate prospect.

Flea markets

Flea markets are another wonderful place to search for old watches and some of my best finds have come from these. I usually go around flea markets asking every person who is selling antiques or collectibles if they have brought any old watches with them that day. Many of these dealers and vendors keep the good stuff hidden out of sight and only bring it out if someone asks or seems interested.

I once found a 1940s vintage Vacheron Constantin man's wristwatch at a flea market for $20. I also bought a nice early 1960s automatic-wind Swiss "Zodiac" watch with day, date and moon phase complications for only $2 because it wasn't in the best condition. I sold it two weeks later and made a profit of $295.

Don't forget to bring cards with you, with your name and number on them, to hand out to the dealers and vendors who left their "good watches" at home. Also, get there early. I cannot count the times when I've heard, "You're the fifth person to ask me about old watches this morning." Many times the regulars who sell at these venues keep watches they have come across in their travels between flea marts stashed away just to show to you when you come around, if it's one of the local affairs you frequent.

Also keep an eye out for vintage watch bands, watchcases, parts or pieces, for they always come in handy at some point for restoration purposes or "trading stock" to other watch prospectors.

Thrift stores

Thrift stores, like the Salvation Army and Goodwill, are good places to check for vintage watches. At first, I was reluctant to go into these places because I figured all the good stuff was gleaned by the people in the back room or the members of the staff who went out and picked up the items at the collection points. However, old stuff attracts other old stuff, and sure enough, I have found good buys at these stores on occasion, such as an early 1970s Swiss Omega automatic "Cosmic" wristwatch in original condition. It even had the original Omega leather band on it with the factory-signed buckle still in place. Since it was not working, it was priced at $1. That particular watch needed some expert repair work to get it back into proper running condition, but after I invested some time and money into it, I realized a profit of $190 after I sold it to a gentleman in Switzerland who was the high bidder in an eBay auction.

Garage sales

Of course, garage sales are also a great place to find hidden treasures. If I don't see any older watches in a particular garage sale, I will always inform the person having the sale that I am interested in old-time, wind-up-type watches. Many times the people will have granddad's old railroad watch wrapped up in a sock somewhere in a dresser drawer. They won't even think to bring it out to a garage sale. Garage sale prices are also generally lower than flea market or thrift store prices.

Estate sales

I have found bargains at estate sales, when family and friends run the sale. But, as a rule, if professionals are hired, they are usually aware of vintage and antique watch values. However, sometimes when there is to be a huge estate sale and there is just too much stuff, an old watch may not be

Bovet Swiss chronometer,
$125-$175.

researched thoroughly and may be under-priced. Of course, being there early helps in finding any deals. If you contact the people who provide estate liquidation services, they can put you on their mailing list and keep you informed of upcoming estate sales where watches are present. They might even let you have the first look at them.

Auction houses

Live auctions are also a place to find old watches of value. If you decide to attend one, be sure to give yourself plenty of time to preview the items up for auction, prior to the sale. But always remember—knowledge is power. You have to do your due diligence and study the subject of watch collecting. If you can glance at a box full of watches and know the approximate retail value of a particular piece, and know it to be 10 times the starting bid price, that is power and you can use it accordingly.

Upscale auction houses, such as Sotheby's and Christie's, know the current values of timepieces, and in many cases, set the values for the market. You get to see nicer pieces, but the prices are higher. I am not an expert in this area, but if money is not an issue, these upscale auction houses are wonderful places to view fabulous vintage watches. In the past, I have been on their mailing lists and have received beautiful color brochures and booklets describing upcoming auctions of fine timepieces. These make wonderful reference materials, even if you can't make the auctions.

Antiques shops

Antiques shops have been, for me, anyway, great places to find old watches and I have found many good and fair deals. It is hard to be an expert in everything out there that is collectible or has value as an antique, and dealers only know so much about everything in their shops. Antiques dealers also have connections with auctioneers, estate liquidators, junk dealers and so on. If they know you are a serious buyer, they will keep their eyes open for you. Antiques collectives are an even greater resource because there are so many dealers under one roof. In recent years, the cost of running an antiques store has become too much for many dealers, so some band together to form collectives and rent out different sized floor areas in their shops, and even rent small glass showcase space. Some of these collectives are huge. There can be 50 different dealers selling merchandise in the same store and putting out old watches they've found.

The Internet

A person can spend days on the Internet finding Web pages of people who deal in watches, auctions on watches, histories of watches, new watches, vintage watches and so on. There are also chat rooms where you can learn more about watch collecting and perhaps make a contact to track down a special watch or part. One of the biggest boons to watch lovers is eBay. On any given day, you can find in excess of 120,000 watches up for auction on this site.

Bradley commando watch, **$10-$15.**

The following are some tips I've discovered while trying to uncover watch deals. It all boils down to the search. When you go to eBay and type the word "watch" in the search title, you will come up with more than 100,000 watch auctions at any given time. This is where most sellers and buyers go. If you enter the word "wristwatch" in the search title, you will get only around 12,000 auctions that come up. Congratulations! You have just stepped ahead of thousands of other people searching for deals. Most people just enter the one word "watch" in their search, kick back, and see what is out there. The same goes for "pocketwatch," but if you type in "pocket watch," a lot more auctions will come up than if you just put in the one word. On eBay, the secret is to find auctions that few other watch prospectors have found. Also, the early bird gets the watches. Try searching for watch auctions that have just been recently listed, instead of the auctions just getting ready to end. You might be able to contact the seller and buy it early before 300 other vintage watch fans discover it.

eBay is not the only site on the Web to find vintage watches, so don't limit yourself. Sotheby's is a great place to discover watch auctions. It has a wide variety and you can always count on finding exotic and rare timepieces on its site. Christie's auction site is another wonderful place to visit for treasures. When you are ready to locate the finest watches for your collection, consider contacting Antiquorum, world-class auctioneers of fine timepieces with offices in Geneva, Milan, Moscow, Paris, Hong Kong, New York, Shanghai, Munich, London and Tokyo. Besides going to one of its auctions in person, you can also view and purchase watches online through its Web auctions: www.antiquorum.com.

The National Association of Watch and Clock Collectors

The National Association of Watch and Clock Collectors in Columbia, Pa., is an excellent organization to belong to and I highly recommend you join. The knowledge you gain and contacts made from being a member are well worth the yearly dues you pay to join. The various chapters of the NAWCC have regular local meetings and special regional events all over the country, and overseas as well. The organization also has a great Internet site at www.nawcc.org. Whether you attend local events, travel to regional meets, or read through its bi-monthly publications, the "NAWCC Bulletin" and the "Mart," your horological world will be enhanced immeasurably. The NAWCC also has The National Watch & Clock Museum and a library and research center.

American Watchmakers-Clockmakers Institute

The American Watchmakers-Clockmakers Institute in Harrison, Ohio, is a not-for-profit trade association. AWCI is dedicated to the advancement of its members and their professions through educational and technical services. You do not have to be a watchmaker to join the AWCI. It is a great association for those interested in the restoration aspect of watch collecting. The AWCI has an informative monthly publication, "The Horological Times," which contains features written by recognized experts dealing with the techniques of servicing and repairing watches, clocks and the functional characteristics of mechanical, electronic and antique timepieces. This, combined with a large classified section and regular watch industry news, provides a great resource for all horologists. The AWCI also has a movement bank/material search network. The American Watchmakers-Clockmakers Institute is the place to start for anyone who is considering becoming a watchmaker or repair person. They have an Academy of Watchmaking, bench courses, and a certification program.

I am a member of AWCI and highly recommend the association. It is the perfect source for locating watchmakers in your area and tracking down parts and information. The AWCI has an educational library and a museum. You can visit its great Web site, too, at www.awci.com.

Before: A Precision-auto wind Gruen, circa 1960s, in as-found condition, with a broken crystal and dirty case.

Condition is what matters

At some point after you have made the decision to search for watch treasure, you will need to acquire a few basic "tools of the trade." When I'm out prospecting, I always carry my small "watch inspection kit" in a belt pouch that contains the following items: One good pair of tweezers, one rubber vacuum case opener for pocket watch (screw back) cases, one watchcase opening knife (for wrist and pocket watches), one decent loupe for magnification, and a few small plastic bags to hold timepieces. Armed with these few tools, you can inspect most pre-1960 timepieces.

After: The same Gruen, after the crystal was replaced and the case cleaned.

Now you are ready to check out your first stash of newly acquired watches. Get a feel for handling them and inspecting their tops and bottoms, sides and ends. At this point, you can start to develop your "extra sensory perception" while attempting to understand what this little machine went through while strapped on the wrist of, or bounced around in the pocket of, its previous owner. Use all of your senses—this will come in handy when out in the field—and look at the overall condition of the watch. Did its owner take good care of it? Was it abused, thrashed, crashed, scratched and dropped? Is it ticking? Is it tocking? Is it humming? Is it silent? Does it rattle? Does it have apparent moisture inside the crystal? Go ahead and start grading them on a scale of 1 to 10 (10 being the highest). This is good practice for when you are out in the field, since you will need to access the condition of timepieces quickly, and occasionally not under the best circumstances—inadequate lighting, minimal tools available for inspection, time constraints, etc. After checking out as many watches as you have on hand at home, you will be ready to go out searching.

It has been said that the three most important things to consider when buying, selling or appraising real estate are "location, location, location." Well, where vintage watches are concerned, you can say "condition, condition, condition" as being the most important considerations. When you are contemplating buying a watch, you must ask yourself over and over, "What is the true state that this timepiece is in, at present?" You must study the watch closely and ascertain its accurate condition. Is it in average condition? Is it in mint condition? How do I tell?

Visual and mechanical condition

When you examine a watch, look at the dial (the face), and get a feel for what the watch has been through. Ask questions from the owner and try to learn the history of the piece. Let the watch "speak to you." A fellow watch fanatic, collector, dealer, buyer, seller, friend of mine once said when I showed him one I had for sale, "The watch just doesn't speak to me." He is so right in thinking this way. You need to reach out with your sixth sense sometimes when contemplating buying a watch and get the feel of it. This is especially true if you're going to be bidding on one, or you need to make a quick decision when in a buying situation. Or, when you are on "the excitement plan" with your credit card in hand, eyes glazed over with anticipation, and your heart is beating way over 9,000 rpm! Remember, it is very easy to buy a watch, but sometimes it can be very hard to resell it, especially if you bought high (high price and high on the idea of owning it), or didn't eyeball it closely.

What does the dial say? If your sixth sense is foggy, then tune up your other five senses to examine the watch. Is the dial an original one? This is of utmost importance to collectors, for in the past it was a common practice for watchmakers to send the dial off to be refinished, if it had even a little wear, when the watch came in for a service. The watchmaker made a little extra money and the customer now had a watch that looked brand new. If it's a Swiss watch, does it say "Switzerland," "Swiss" or "Swiss Made" on the bottom of the dial? Does the dial have any stains, discoloration, cracks, chips, scratches, dings or dents? Is the paint faded or partly missing? If the dial is enamel, does it have any hairline cracks that can be seen with the naked eye or under magnification? If the dial has been restored in the past and is not the original, how does the refinish work look? Was it a quality refinish job? Is it crisp? Lines straight and wording correct?

Move next to the hands. Are they straight? Do the hands match and are they original? Look at the center where the hands attach. Is it all scratched up? Do they look like they have been taken off and put back on 50 times? Examine the crown (the button used for winding and setting). Does it look to be an original one, or does it have the watch manufacturer's logo or name on it? Does it sit up against the body of the case straight and close? Does it wobble out of round when you turn it (bent stem or crown tube)? Turn the crown. What does it feel like? Is it a smooth-winding feel? When winding the mainspring does it skip or feel scratchy (winding mechanism wheels or pinion teeth problems)? Do you wind and wind and wind but never seem to get it fully wound (mainspring broken or slipping)? Pull the crown out into the setting position. Does it stay pulled out smartly, or slip back in (broken setting bridge)? Now turn the crown for setting the hands and notice how it feels. Is it hard to turn the crown or does it turn too freely (too tight or too loose cannon pinion)? Do the hands line up correctly? Do the hands hit the dial or touch the roof of the crystal? What condition is the crystal in? Is it plastic or glass? Tap it on your front teeth. With practice, you can tell the difference between the two. Plastic crystals can usually have their scratches all polished out. Glass ones are harder to restore when all scratched and chipped. Any cracks or breaks in the crystal will allow moisture and dust inside the dial area, and will need to be replaced.

Next, check out the case. Does it look original to the movement? What material is it made of? Solid gold, gold filled, gold plated, platinum, silver, nickel silver, stainless steel, chrome-plated base metal? Visually, what condition is it in? Note any wear through the plating, or brass showing through;

notice any dents, dings, scratches, pitting, bent or misshapen areas. If it is a pocket watch with a threaded back and bezel, are they cross-threaded or do they screw on and off smoothly? If the case has a snap-fit bezel and back, check for scratches and marring that an errant case opener knife left. If it is a hunter-case pocket watch, with a front and back cover, check to see if the bezel is in place and is the correct one. If you are examining a wristwatch case, look to see if the fits are close between the body and bezel, and the back and body. Check to see if the lugs (the thin metal rods used for attaching the straps) are straight.

If it is a runner, listen to the movement. Does it sound strong and steady no matter what position you hold it in? Is the movement loose inside the case—does it rattle? If it is an automatic winding-type watch, can you hear the rotor when it spins around? Is it a smooth sound or can you hear the rotor hitting the case back or the movement plate? If the watch is a complicated one, have the owner show you the different functions and how they work. Ask the seller if it is OK to open the back up and visibly check out the movement. If you are able to get that far into the watch, look on the underside of the case back for screw- head marks where movement case screws may have backed out and worn into the case. Also look under the case back for watchmaker marks, as they can tell you a story of how often the movement was serviced through the years.

Inspect the condition of the movement and look for rust spots, especially on the hairspring. Examine the balance wheel area. Does the balance wheel turn freely and smoothly? Does it wobble? Look closely at the screw heads holding the movement together. Look at the slots in the screw heads where the screwdriver blade fits. Are they all in good shape, or have they been marked up by being removed and replaced too many times by careless repair people? There are a lot of "hackers" out in the

A "hacker" attempt at watch repair ruined this fine old Howard. Note the upper right-hand corner.

watch world, who, after reading a couple of repair manuals and looking at a few pictures, believe that they are master watchmakers. I have opened many a fine watch only to find screwdriver skid marks across a bridge or plate, and screw heads broken and messed up.

Many watch collectors are only interested in the outward appearance of their vintage watch. Whether it functions properly is a secondary consideration. I must say that the condition of the outward appearance is probably the most important factor in most peoples' minds, but you

should get in the habit of grading the watch as a whole. If you have not yet established a relationship with a qualified watch-repair person, seek one out as soon as possible. Once you have found a competent watchmaker to work with, he or she will assist you in keeping your vintage watches in top condition. Contact the American Watchmakers-Clockmakers Institute for help in finding a watchmaker in your area.

When buying a watch, you can use the following rating scale to help place a value on the timepiece:

10. Positively mint—NOS, unused, factory fresh and still in the original box.
9. Mint +—Pristine, in original box, perhaps slightly or rarely used, but looks as if it was never used.
8. Mint—In original condition with only little use and no scratches, marks or wear.
7. Near mint—In original condition, used but with only faint marks or wear.
6. Fine +—Taken good care of, with original parts used in any repairs or restoration. Little scratches, marks or wear.
5. Fine—Crisp with only minor wear, marks and scratches. Still has original case, dial may have had quality restoration done, has original movement.
4. Average—Wear from normal use for its age, but still with original case, dial (may have been refinished) and movement. Normal dings, wear marks and scratches expected from daily use.
3. Fair—Well used, and may not have the original case, dial or movement.
2. Poor—Broken, not working, parts missing, well worn, but restorable.
1. Junk—Totally worn out, damaged, rust, "parts watch" only.

Restoration

When you find a vintage watch worthy of restoration, you must consider all of what that entails. Let us say that you discover a wristwatch in 4 grade (average) condition, with a badly discolored dial. To restore the dial or not to restore the dial, that is the question.

Generally speaking, a dial has to be fairly well gone before I refinish it. Collectors always prefer a watch with an original dial. However, if it is just plain ugly, then get it refinished. Sometimes it is a tough call and a lot of the decision rests with what you plan to do with the watch after restora-

A 1930s Bulova with badly rusted hands and dial.

The same 1930s Bulova, with dial restored and hands replaced.

A damaged 1890s enamel pocket watch dial.

The same enamel pocket watch dial, after the author repaired the damaged areas.

tion. If you enjoy the look of the watch and plan to wear it, then getting the dial redone is a question of personal preference. If you obtained the watch with the desire to resell it, then you might consider cleaning up the case, crystal, and movement, but leave the decision to restore the dial to the next owner. However, if the dial is too ugly, there might not be a next owner anytime soon.

You must be careful and examine the dial closely to see if it will stand up to a light cleaning. Your watchmaker will know best what to recommend as far as dial cleaning goes. Usually you're better off not trying to clean it. Enamel dials are easier to have cleaned, as the enamel has been kiln fired onto metal and the lettering and numbers are more stable. Repairs can also be made on enamel dials, but keep in mind that enamel is like glass and you must be careful with them. Hairline cracks can grow and chunks can fall off if these dials are mistreated. A huge percentage of vintage wrist and pocket watches with enamel dials have pronounced or faint hairline cracks in them. It is exciting to find one of these fine old watches with a perfect dial on it. Enamel dials with hairlines can be placed in an "ultrasonic cleaner" and the hairlines will disappear. However, they will return as soon as dust and dirt start settling in the cracks again. Examine them closely with a good loupe to determine if they are free of hairlines or not.

Many times, a watch just needs a good polish and a new crystal to look new again. To restore vintage watchcases, there are watchcase repair experts who can re-plate gold-plated cases, repair broken hinges, make new bezels, fix holes, dings and deep scratches. Solid gold cases are easier to polish up and restore than gold-plated or gold-filled ones. Gold-filled cases are the next best thing to solid gold (gold

filled is like an Oreo cookie lying on its side; there is base metal inside, usually brass, with thick plates of gold on the outsides). In the past, pocket watchcases were sometimes marked "5 Years," "10 Years," "Warranted 20 Years," etc. This is an indication of how thick the gold plates were when the case was made. Can you imagine anything warranted for 20 years nowadays? It's amazing that these gold-filled cases were made so well that the manufacturer could guarantee they would hold up for 10 or 20 years. Actually, most of these vintage gold-filled cases lasted many times longer than their warranty before any of the gold wore off to reveal the brass sandwiched inside. Rolled gold plate, sometimes stamped on cases as R.G.P., is the same as gold-fill, except the gold plating is thinner than gold-filled cases. The R.G.P. watchcases did not hold up as long as the gold filled ones, but would last better than the next category, which is the gold-electroplated case. These cases just have a few microns of gold plating. Great care has to be used when polishing and restoring them to original finish.

Some watches just need a good surface cleaning and polishing, such as this 1950's Elgin found in good running condition.

Restoration of gold-filled and rolled gold-plated cases is tricky business. On wristwatch cases, the sharp edges usually wear through first—the corners, high spots, edges of the bezel and back, under the lugs, and also the tips of the lugs are the first to go. The case repairer must solder and/or re-plate the case. Depending on the severity of the wear, many times it just isn't worth the time and money to fully restore a badly worn-through gold-filled or R.G.P. case.

A 1950s Bulova with a badly discolored dial.

Restoring the movement of a vintage watch depends on the age of the timepiece and availability of parts. If the movement just needs a cleaning and oiling, this is to be considered standard maintenance. If the movement has broken or rusted parts, you will need an esti-

The restored Bulova, circa 1950s, gold filled, diamond dial, after dial restoration.

mate for repair and restoration from a competent watchmaker or repair person. Watches manufactured prior to the 1950s might not be shock-protected and must be examined for balance-staff problems. If it was manufactured prior to the 1940s, it definitely wasn't shock-protected, since few watches had this feature prior to that time. When a watch is dropped or shocked severely, the balance staff and the crystal are the first to break. When examining a watch, see that the balance turns while the watch is held in various positions. A watch with a broken balance staff may work in one position, but not in another. A watch that is old or one that is rare, where only a few were originally made or have survived, can usually have parts made for it if none are available. This is most always an expensive and time-consuming process.

Suffice it to say that the more you inspect and handle these little machines, the better you will become at knowing what to look for, and the better you will become at judging their true condition, condition, condition.

Buying and selling

First, let me warn you right now of the problem of fakes in the market. Most of us have seen the cheap fake Rolex watches that are out there by the millions. If you are not sure how a fake Rolex measures up to the real McCoy, go to your local Rolex dealer and ask to see a few.

Fake Rolexes hurt dealers' businesses and I'm sure they wouldn't mind letting you handle a couple of real ones. That way you can get the feel and heft and notice the craftsmanship and attention to detail that goes into making each one. Newer fakes are easy to spot once you have spent the time checking out the real thing.

However, now that I've said that, a friend of mine, in his travels, came across a fake made to look exactly like a 1940s vintage Rolex. These are hard for the rookie to identify and you must be careful. Always buy from a reputable dealer and remember to pay attention to detail and work-manship when inspecting the piece. There are some really good fakes of Omega watches out there and I myself was nearly fooled by one until I removed the back to inspect the movement. The outside of the watch, including the dial, looked authentic and the finish was relatively crisp. Once I peeked in the back, though, I knew it was fake. Be careful you don't get stung.

Buying

If you are just starting to collect vintage watches, it is a good idea to concentrate on just one kind of watch: American 21-jewel pocket watches or automatic-wind wristwatches, or just one brand/maker of watches, such as Hamilton, Waltham, Longines, Omega, Gruen, Mido, Vacheron Constantin, etc. This way you can become fairly knowledgeable about your particular favorite watches in a relatively short amount of time. In my early collecting days, I would buy anything and everything as long as I thought I was getting a deal. After ending up with drawers full of every kind of watch, in every kind of condition (mostly broken), I decided to be a little pickier. If you run into good deals on watches that are not the kind you collect, you can always use them for "trading stock" to other dealers or watchmakers, who are always looking for parts. Just be careful not to buy everything you come across or you can spend a lot of money and not have as much to show for it. It is a far better investment to buy a couple mint or near-mint timepieces than two dozen below-average-condition clunkers.

When you have discovered a watch you want, you must truthfully ask yourself a few questions. How you answer these questions will help you decide how much you're willing to spend on any given watch. What are you buying the watch for? Are you going to keep it and add the piece to your collection? Are you going to resell the watch? If you are going to sell it, are you going to sell it at a wholesale or retail price?

When you ask the seller how much they want for the watch and they say, "I was hoping you could tell me what it is worth," you will have to do some quick calculations in your head. If you are going to keep the watch for your own collection, you can pay a little more for it, as you don't have to think about turning a profit. If you plan to resell it, it is good to remember to "buy low and sell high." Until I really studied the market, I used to "buy high and sell low." Then I discovered it was more fun the other way. Knowledge is the key.

When you are speaking to someone on the phone about a watch and, after finding out what kind it is (gent's, lady's) and who the maker is, here are some questions to ask:

1. Does the watch wind up and does it run? Can you pull the crown (winder) out and set the hands?

2. What color is the dial (face) and what condition is it in? Is it the original dial or has it been restored/refinished at some point in the past? What is written (printed) on the dial? If it is a Swiss watch, it should have "Swiss," "Swiss Made," or "Switzerland" printed at the bottom of the dial, below the six o'clock position.

3. What material is the case made of—stainless steel, yellow gold, white gold, gold filled, rolled gold plate, gold electroplate, silver, nickel, chrome plate?

4. What condition is the case in? Any dents? Dings? Scratches? Worn spots? Is there any engraving on the watch?

5. What is the history of the piece?

6. How would the overall condition and appearance of the watch be rated? Average? Fine? Mint?

7. What is the asking price?

Making an offer on a vintage watch can be an art in itself. You can get people mad at you, embarrass yourself to no end and help create some bad vibes if you don't proceed with caution. If you are at an antiques shop where the price is already fixed, you cannot expect to do much bargaining. However, if you are buying over the phone from an ad you placed, or at a flea market, garage sale or estate sale, you might be able to negotiate the price. If I ask the seller how much they want for the watch and they say they don't know and ask me what it's worth, I tell them exactly what I know to be true.

Let's say, for instance, it is a circa early 1960s stainless steel Omega "Seamaster" automatic-wind wristwatch that needs servicing, as it has sat in a drawer for 20 years. You have judged the watch to be in the #6, Fine + condition. In this scenario, the watch is working OK and doesn't need any parts; it just needs a cleaning, oiling and polishing. In this case, I will tell them their watch, when serviced and in excellent running condition, is worth around $295 to a collector. But I also tell them I have to put some time, effort and money into the piece to bring it up to standard, and then will have to search out a collector who loves the watch enough to part with $295 for it. Since we also live in good old capitalist America, I also note I need to make a little profit for my efforts and can therefore offer them $125 for their watch. After I explain this to the person, nine times out of 10 they say they understand I've got to make a little something on the deal and my offer sounds like a fair price.

Stainless steel watches are a good bet to buy, such as this refinished/restored Gubelin, circa 1940s, **$100-$300.**

What to buy

So what's hot? Generally, for wristwatches, I believe you can never go wrong by picking up good quality stainless steel men's pieces, especially brand name automatic-wind wristwatches. Unusually shaped wristwatches, watches with complications (day, date, chronograph functions, moon phase, alarm, world time, repeater, etc.), limited-edition pieces (watches the factory didn't make many of), early wristwatches from the 1910s and 1920s, and rose gold (pink gold) wristwatches are your best bets. Stainless steel wristwatches from the 1940s through the 1960s seem to be real hot collectibles.

For pocket watches, look for early examples of the top American and Swiss makers (low serial numbers), American railroad-grade and railroad-approved 16- and 18-size pocket watches, hunter case watches, pocket watches with multicolored dials and high-grade Swiss pocket watches, especially ones made in the 1960s and 1970s, which are rather hard to find.

As for ladies' watches, what is highly collectible seems to be wide open for debate. At present, tiny ladies' watches from the 1940s through the 1960s do not seem to be highly sought after, and larger watches have become more popular with ladies now. Higher grade, name-brand women's wristwatches such as Movado, Longines, Omega, Rolex, Cartier, Vacheron Constantin, etc., are always popular no matter what size, especially if they are unusual in some way or have diamonds or other stones set into their cases. I like early (larger pieces) 1910s or 1920s Elgin, Hamilton and Gruen ladies' watches, especially if they have enamel on them.

Ladies' pocket watches and pendant watches are a bit fragile and rather high-maintenance items, if you are going to bounce them around in everyday use. For this reason, I don't see a huge interest in this area. Still, the enamel ladies' pieces are little works of art and are sought after for their beauty. The whole area of collectible ladies' watches is a huge market waiting to catch fire. It seems that men are the biggest collectors of watches and have been for some time. I would love to see more women

Pocket-watch collectors should be on the lookout for early pieces. Aurora Watch Co., circa 1884, first-year production, GF 18 size 15J OF, **$295- $495.**

Women's watches made by name-brand companies are always popular. Cartier "Roadster," ladies stainless steel, 1990s, **$2,500.**

get excited about collecting the smaller timepieces, as they are truly marvels of miniature engineering, craftsmanship and beauty. The watch factories across the world have, since they began mass production, employed thousands of women to assemble the watches. It is high time the ladies started buying back, and collecting, what they themselves helped to create.

Selling

The following are some points to consider if you want to sell a watch. Are you going to guarantee the watch or are you going to use the old flea-market rule of "20 seconds or 20 feet?" In other words, you'll only guarantee the piece for 20 seconds after the buyer purchases it or until the buyer gets 20 feet away from you with it; after that, they're on their own. If you use this rule, you will need to inform potential buyers that perhaps the watch has been lying in an old drawer for 42 years and, although it might tick for a bit, it isn't going to tock and you are not guaranteeing it to keep good time. Inform buyers they should consider having it serviced should they want to wear it; or, in the case of pocket watches, carry it.

If you have spent time and money going through the watch and have it all polished and running great, let the buyer know this also. Explain to them all that was done to the timepiece—overhaul, services, parts replaced, etc. If you have had the watch fully serviced and can now guarantee it to run and keep time, the selling price should reflect this. Some collectors would rather take care of the servicing on their own (they do it themselves or take it to their trusted watchmaker) as this is part of their collecting fun.

Where to sell your watch

As a rule, collectors pay the highest prices for watches. They are going to keep the watches they purchase and don't have to worry so much about saving room for profit when buying them. Watch dealers, of course, need to buy low and sell high to stay in business; therefore, you won't generally get as much for your watches from them. However, you might sit on your watch for a long time waiting to find the right collector to come by and fall in love with it. Dealers are in touch

with many collectors and you might be able to turn your watches over faster through them.

To sell watches, you need to go where the dealers and collectors go: the Internet, AWCI, NAWCC, antiques shops, antiques shows, auction houses, networking, advertising, etc. You can rent a space in an antiques collective to display and sell your timepieces. Most of these collectives rent space in their showcases and are perfect spots for selling small items like watches. You can also offer your items to dealers who already have showcase spots set up with watches. Joining the AWCI and the NAWCC, and attending local and regional shows, are excellent avenues for selling watches. Plus, it's a lot of fun.

The Internet is a great avenue for selling your watches, since you are placing them in front of thousands of watch lovers and potential buyers. You can join an online auction service and in no time at all conduct your own watch auctions.

There are also many Web sites set up by vintage watch dealers and you can contact them directly about selling your timepieces, as they are always looking to acquire more items for their businesses. Many times these dealers are also into the watch-repair business, and so you can offer them watches that are not running or that need restoration. You can list your watches online with big auction houses such as Sotheby's, if you don't mind paying them a percentage of the sale. Antiquorum is a wonderful auction service, as it specializes in fine timepieces and is one of the world's leading auctioneers in the field of horology. If you want to display and sell watches from your collection, you can look into setting up your own vintage-watch Web site. There are Web-based "chat rooms" for sharing information, too.

I have successfully sold hundreds of watches over the years through NAWCC, setting up spots in collectives, and on the Internet. Wherever you go to sell your watches, remember this: Always describe the watch accurately and truthfully. Don't sell any hidden surprises to people. If you don't know everything about a piece, then tell prospective buyers that. Point out any known flaws so the buyer knows exactly what they're getting. The golden rule applies here. The reward in doing this is obvious—people appreciate the honesty and they will become repeat customers.

Watch Values and Identification

This book is meant to be a guide for you in the search for the current market value of your watch. This is not the last word on the value of watches, and it is not meant to be the complete "watch bible and encyclopedia" on the subject.

The values of vintage watches change with trends in the market, the state of our economy, tastes in personal attire, what era in time happens to be cool and trendy this season, etc.

All I do know is that values of vintage watches have done nothing but go up the past few decades and I don't see that slowing down.

Unless otherwise noted, the watch prices listed are for watches in good running condition, with all parts in place, band and crystal, etc., and are for the most part retail prices and what you would expect to pay in antiques shops, vintage/estate jewelry establishments, from professional watch dealers, or fine auction houses.

I have listed price ranges of most watches in average to near-mint condition. If your watch is in need of repairs or is in less-than-average condition, the value of the timepiece will be less than the average price to reflect some of the cost of repairs and restoration.

If the watch in question is in mint condition, then the sky is the limit and you can name your price. The limiting factors are condition, rarity and demand.

Here is an example of how much of a moving target watch prices can be: A watch

Abbreviations used:
GF = Gold filled
GP = Gold plated
HC = Hunter case
J = Jewel
LS = Lever set
OF = Open face
PS = Pin set
RR = Railroad

Bulova pocket watch, circa 1920s, GF engraved edge and bail, 17J fancy metal dial, **$195-$395.**

dealer friend of mine rents a spot in a large antiques collective in one town, owns a nice estate jewelry/watch shop in another town and also operates an upscale estate jewelry shop in yet a third town. He placed a vintage watch for sale in the antiques collective and priced it at $200, which is what, in his experience, was a good retail price. The watch sat for months with no activity, so he reduced the price to $150—still no activity. So, he took the watch out of the antiques store, placed it in his estate jewelry/watch shop, and put a price of $295 on it. There it sat for another long period of time with no interested buyer. He then took the watch to his third location, the upscale estate jewelry shop, where he changed the price tag on it to $695. The watch sold in two weeks! What do you suppose he is going to ask for a similar watch if he should acquire one and put it up for sale? This is a perfect example, albeit an unusual one, of how watch prices can be moving targets.

In another example, I had a Hamilton Coronado wristwatch from the 1930s that sold for $1,000 more than I or my watch dealer friends thought that it would. It was one of the more scarce and collectible of watches and much in demand, I learned through the experience.

Some watches are also worth more on the West Coast than on the East Coast, so you must do research and get information from different resources to get an accurate value for a given watch.

Hamilton is a top name in watches. Hamilton "Assymetic" electric, 1950s, **$350.**

If you think a price is too high on a watch you plan to buy, ask your-self how hard it would be to find another one in its condition.

Here is a small list of the names of watches and watch manufacturers to keep your eye out for: Agassiz, Alpina, Angelus, Assmann, Audemars Piguet, Ball Watch Co., Baume & Mercier, J.W. Benson, Benrus, Blancpain, Breguet, Breitling, Bucherer, Bulova, Cartier, Chopard, Columbus Watch Co., Croton, Cyma, Dent, Ditisheim, Doxa, Ebel, Eberhard, Ekegren, Elgin, Eterna, Favre Leuba, Gallet, Geneve, Girard Perregaux, Glasshutte, Glycine, Goering, Golay, Gotham, Gruen, Gubelin, Hafis, Hamilton, Hampden, Harwood, Hebdomas, Helbros, Heuer, E. Howard & Co., E. Howard Watch Co. (Keystone), Huguenin, Illinois Watch Co., Ingersoll, E. Ingraham Co., International Watch Co., Junghans, Jules Jurgensen, Juvenia, Lancaster Watch Co., A. Lange & Sohne, LeCoultre, Lemania, Longines, Lucien Piccard, C. H. Meylan, Mido, Minerva, Montbrillant, Moser Cie., Movado, Ulysse Nardin, New England Watch Co., New Haven, New York Standard, Nivada, Non-Magnetic Watch Co., Ollendorf, Omega, Patek Philippe, Patria, Piaget, Pierce, Pulsar, Rado, Record, Roamer, Rockford Watch Co., Rolex, Roskopf, Rotary, Sandoz, Seiko, Seth Thomas, Shreve & Co., South Bend Watch Co., Tavannes, Tiffany & Co., Tissot, Trenton Watch Co., Universal, United States Watch Co., Vacheron Constantin, Vulcain, Wakmann, Waltham Watch Co. (American Waltham Watch Co.), Waterbury Watch Co., Westclox, Wittnauer, Wyler, Zenith, and Zodiac.

The watches listed in this guide are just a sampling of the millions of timepieces that have been bought or sold by collectors, watch dealers, antiques dealers, Internet traders, and auction houses. They will provide you with a good place to start for finding a value for your watches.

Pocket Watches

Many early watch manufacturers decorated their watch dials and cases with locomotives and other railroad scenes. This, however, does not denote them to be true railroad grade or railroad-approved timepieces. Railroad standards were implemented in the 1890s and had nothing to do with the decoration on the case or the dial of the watch.

Watches are listed alphabetically by maker.

Agassiz 17 ligne Swiss chrono-graph, 14k, **$1,500-$2,000.**

Agassiz Watch Co., circa 1920, 21J 43mm nickel case, power reserve indicator, center seconds stop/start feature, **$2,000-$3,000.** *Photo courtesy of Antiquorum.*

Agassiz World Time, circa 1945, 14k, **$5,000-$7,000.** *Photo courtesy of Antiquorum.*

BALL WATCH CO.

Founded in the early 1890s in Cleveland, Ohio, by Webb C. Ball, this company is famous for its marketing of high-grade railroad watches produced by companies such as Elgin, Hamilton, Illinois and Waltham.

The company's pocket watches are highly prized by collectors today.

Ball 16 size official railroad standard, 21J RR, GF case, **$400-$900.**

Ball dial, commercial standard (Swiss), 16 size, dial only, **$50-$150.**

Ball 999B, circa 1900s, 21J 16 size, **$695-$1,195.**

COLUMBUS WATCH CO.

Founded in 1882, this Columbus, Ohio, company was sold in 1903 to establish the South Bend Watch Co. in Indiana.

Columbus Railway King, circa 1899, 18 size 16J Railway King movement, nickel case, Sidewinder, **$300-$600.**

Railway King movement view.

Columbus Railway King, circa 1899, GF HC with Railway King dial, 16J, **$300-$600.**

Movement view of the Railway King.

DUDLEY WATCH CO.

Started in the early 1920s, this company in Lancaster, Pa., produced a limited number of pocket watches in which the bridges took the form of Masonic symbols.

Dudley Masonic, circa late 1940s, 12 size, third model, display back, YGF, **$1,500-$2,500.**

ELGIN NATIONAL WATCH CO.

Founded in 1864, this
Elgin, Ill., company
produced more jeweled
watches than any other
in America during its
more than 90-year his-
tory. The company
made watches ranging
from low-end all the
way up through to its
famous high-quality
railroad grades. These
railroad pocket watches
are highly sought after
as is the company's
collectible Art Deco
wristwatches.

Elgin "Dexter Street," circa 1873, 10 size, KW KS, 14k,
$395-$595.

Dexter Street movement.

Dexter Street case.

Elgin 18 size, circa 1879, sweep second/ doctor's watch, GF, **$395-$795.**

Movement view of the doctor's watch.

Elgin 17J LS, circa 1886, GF box hinge case, engraved horse, **$295-$595.**

Elgin 11J 6 size, circa 1886, 14k HC, **$295-$795.**

Elgin 14k engraved bird motif case of the watch above.

Elgin circa 1888 6 size, GF HC LS, **$295-$595.**

Movement view of the watch above.

Elgin case front, left, and case back of the watch shown above.

Elgin fancy enamel HC, circa 1900s, 14k, 6 size, case, 14k chain with fob, floral motif with petite floral chain to floral ball, original velvet box, **$2,250-$2,750.**

Elgin 21J 16 size, circa 1896, 14k fancy HC, **$695-$1,195.**

Movement #156 of the watch above.

Elgin 7J 0 size, circa 1895, GF HC, **$95-$295.**

Movement view of the watch above.

Fancy engraved case of the watch above.

Elgin Veritas, circa 1901, dual time zone, sterling 21J 18 size, **$395-$795.**

Veritas case.

Veritas movement view.

Elgin RR, circa 1902, grade 270/three-finger bridge, 21J 16 size, nickel case, **$295-$495.**

Movement view of the RR.

Elgin 24-hour military-style dial, circa 1902, 16 size, nickel silver case, **$195-$350.**

The U.S. eagle emblem on the case of the watch at left.

Elgin circa 1903, 18 size, 17J OF, nickel, **$150-$250.**

Engraved case of the Elgin 17J movement.

Elgin 14k multi-colored HC, circa 1904, light blue fancy dial, 15J, **$695-$995.**

Engraved case of the watch above.

Elgin circa 1908, 15J nickel, 18 size,
$125-$225.

Movement view of the watch at left.

Elgin BW Raymond, circa 1908, 19J 18 size,
GF case, double sunk dial, **$175-$375.**

Movement view of the BW Raymond.

Elgin circa 1908, very light green dial, GF 7J 16 size, **$95-$195.**

Elgin circa 1910, 18 size 17J HC, diamond, sapphire, and ruby, **$3,000-$3,500.** *Photo courtesy of Antiquorum.*

Elgin movement view, circa 1910, nickel display case, 17J 18 size, **$95-$225.**

Elgin BW Raymond, circa 1911, 21J 16 size, nickel OF, **$200-$400.**

Elgin multicolored dial, double sunk with yellow and green gold appliqué, 16 size, new-old factory stock, circa 1915, sold for **$750.**

Elgin 15J 16 size, circa 1919, note sub-seconds at 3:00, WGF/metal dial, **$65-$175.**

Elgin Masonic dial, circa 1920s, GF, **$200-$400.**

Elgin circa 1920s, GF pink OF, 12 size, **$295-$495.**

Elgin circa 1920, 15J 12 size, GF OF, **$95- $195.**

Movement view of the watch at left.

Elgin BW Raymond RR, circa 1924, 21J 16 size, GF, up-down indicator, **$795-$1,295.**

Elgin with flip-out stand, circa 1927, 17J 12 size, white gold, **$494-$795.**

Movement view of the watch at left.

Elgin circa 1930s, 7J 16 size, WGF OF, **$125-$200.**

Elgin BW Raymond RR, #571, circa 1940, 16 size, GF, 21J 9 adj., **$200-$500.**

Movement view of the BW Raymond.

Elgin circa 1950, 16 size 17J, GF OF, **$195-$395.**

The 574 movement of the watch at left.

Elgin Swiss, circa 1960s, OF, 16 size, 17J base metal, **$75-$175.**

The movement view of the Swiss.

Elgin Swiss, circa 1950s or 1960s, approximately 0 size, 17J sweep second, GF, antique reproduction, **$95-$195.**

Back view of case (notice shock absorber through window).

Elgin/Montgomery dial RR, 6 size 21J, GF, incorrect bow, **$225-$495.**

Elgin Father Time RR, 16 size 21J movement, **$200-$475.**

Elgin with early images of children on dial, 6 size, chrome case, **$95-$195.**

Elgin PW movement shipping box, circa 1922, 12 size, **$10-$20.**

Watch case company ad inside pocket watch case.

Elgin pocket watch early celluloid advertising piece with Father Time, **$20-$30.**

Watch certification card, circa late 1950s or 1960s, **$5-$10.**

GRUEN WATCH CO.

Founded in the 1870s in Columbus, Ohio, Gruen is famous for its imported Swiss "Guild" movements, and for the "Veri-Thin," "Curvex," and "Doctors" watches.

Gruen Veri-Thin Swiss, circa 1910, fancy engraved metal dial, GF, **$200-$350.**

Gruen Veri-Thin, circa 1920, GF, 17J, pentagon shape, fancy enamel detail, **$195-$495.**

Gruen Veri-Thin original papers.

Gruen Veri-Thin, circa 1920s, 17J, GF, five-sided case, **$175-$475.**

Veri-Thin Movement view.

Gruen Veri-Thin with copper dial, circa 1930s, 15J, GF, **$100-$200.**

Veri-Thin movement view.

Gruen Veri-Thin 14k with pentagonal case, inside movement also shown, 1920s, **$550.**

Gruen Veri-Thin, white gold filled, 1920s, **$150.**

Gruen Veri-Thin, hexagonal case, white gold filled, 1920s, **$200.**

Dietrich Gruen, 18k white gold with enameled pentagonal case, raised gold numbers, 1920s, **$700.**

D. Gruen & Sons Canadian Railroad watch, gold filled case, circa 1908, **$600.**

Gruen Extra, chrome-plated case, 21J movement, made in Madresch, Switzerland, **$250.**

HAMILTON WATCH CO.

Founded in 1892, this Lancaster, Pa., company is regarded by many collectors as the premier watch manufacturer in American history. The company produced high-quality watches and was popular in the railroad industry. The master watchmaker I worked for in the 1970s timed every watch that left the store up against a Hamilton 992B pocket watch that hung on a nail in the repair room.

Hamilton made watch-making history when it introduced its battery-powered wristwatch in 1957. Hamilton railroad pocket watches are sought after by collectors, as are examples from the large wristwatch line that it produced.

Hamilton factory scene, celluloid advertising item, 1900s.

Hamilton circa 1897, Montgomery dial, 24-hour division inside hour chapter, 14k HC, 17J 18 size, **$795-$1,295.**

Inside movement view of the watch above.

The engraved case of the watch above.

Hamilton 946, Parks Jewelers-Dauphine, Manitoba, Canada, circa 1905, 23J 18 size, **$695-$1,195.**

Movement view of the 946.

Hamilton Grade 944, circa 1905, 19J 18 size, five position, display type case, **$275-$575.**

Movement view of the 944.

Hamilton 950, circa 1906, 23J 16 size, movement view, **$795-$1,295.**

Hamilton 992, circa 1909, 21J 16 size, silver case, **$295-$595.**

Inside movement view of the 922.

Hamilton 16 size, circa 1919, 21J, montgomery dial 992, WGF case is marked Hamilton Railroad Model, **$295-$595.**

Hamilton 992 Time King, circa 1919, 21J 16 size, **$295-$595.**

Hamilton Presentation Watch with coin holder fob, circa 1920, 14k, 12 size model 920 23J, **$595-$895.**

Movement view of the Presentation watch, adjusted to five positions, swing-out case.

Hamilton model 950, circa 1932, Montgomery dial, 16 size, 23J, 14k GF, **$1,000-$1,500.**

Movement view of the 950.

Hamilton 992L, circa 1932, very bold dial, 21J 16 size, GF, **$295-$595.**

Movement view of the 922L.

Hamilton Model 992L, circa 1932, 21J 16 size, WGF, signed Ham., case with solid bow, **$395-$895.**

Movement view of the 922L.

Hamilton RR, 992B, circa 1942, 21J 16 size, YGF, signed Ham. case, **$395-$795.**

Movement view of the 922B.

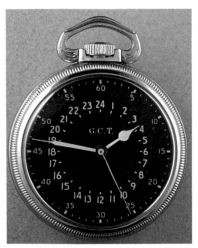

Hamilton 4992B, GCT (Greenwich Civil Time), circa 1942, 22J, chrome case/24-hour black dial, **$395-$595.**

Inside movement view of the 4992B.

Hamilton 992B Railway Special, circa 1942, 21J, GF, two-tone case, **$325-$625.**

Hamilton chronograph/Grade 23, circa WW II, nickel plate, **$295-$495.**

Hamilton Grade 912, circa 1938, 12 size, engraved metal dial, GF, **$75-$175.**

Hamilton military Grade 23 chronograph, circa 1940s, 19J 16 size, unusual refinished white dial, **$295-$495.**

Hamilton, Grade 917 with box, circa 1937, 17J 10 size, GF, **$125-$295.**

28

The Home of **FAITH** *Products*

★ HAMILTON WATCH ★

★

The
MASTERPIECE GROUP

This exclusive group is regarded as altogether worthy of the fine name of Hamilton—the choice of those who are satisfied only with the best.

All watches in this group are high-grade 23-jewel Masterpiece Hamiltons, adjusted to heat, cold and five positions. They have a patent motor barrel, gold train, steel escape wheel, double roller escapement, sapphire pallets, micrometric regulator, Breguet hairspring and Invar bi-metallic compensation balance.

Hamilton Masterpiece Model "C"

Exceptionally beautiful is this newest masterpiece—Model "C." Hand made throughout, in a handsomely engraved case of extra heavy 18K white or green gold. The dial is of sterling silver, satin finish, polished circle outlined in blue enamel. Raised numerals of 18K gold. Consumer price, $250.00.

Hamilton Masterpiece Model "B"

The Model "B" is an exquisite expression of Hamilton accuracy and skill. The case is of 18K extra heavy white or green gold. Hand made throughout, and richly carved. Sterling silver dial, brushed or lined finish with raised numerals of 18K gold. Consumer price, $250.00.

The Hamilton Masterpiece in Platinum

For distinguished visitors and retiring presidents and others deserving of high honor—the Hamilton Platinum Masterpiece is the presentation gift supreme. Here modern art and science meet in a flawless combination of beauty and accuracy. Here is the Hamilton ideal of master craftsmanship.

It is cased entirely in platinum, beautifully hand chased in rich design. The dial of sterling silver has raised numerals of gold. The hands are also of gold. Consumer price, $685.00.

Hamilton
The Watch of Railroad Accuracy

★ ★ ★ ★ ★ ★

Consumers' Prices Only on This Page—For List Prices See Page 35

A vintage Hamilton watch ad for the Masterpiece Group.

HAMPDEN WATCH CO.

Founded in the late 1870s, this Canton, Ohio, company produced watches, the vast majority being pocket type, up until the early 1930s when it was bought by the Soviet Union, which moved the company to that country.

Hampden circa 1891, 6 size, 14k multicolor HC, **$500-$1,000.**

Movement view of the watch above.

The case front of the watch above is in green and pink gold, with a flowers and parrot motif.

Hampden Dueber, circa 1902, 18 size le-ver set base metal case, **$75-$150.**

Lever set movement of the Dueber.

Hampden John Hancock model, circa 1910, 18 size 21J GF HC Ferguson dial, **$2,000-$2,400.** *Photo courtesy of Antiquorum.*

Hampden Molly Stark, circa 1910, 3/0 size 7J, GF hunter case, **$100-$225.**

Movement view of Molly Stark.

Hampden Model 306, circa 1912, GF 15J 12 size, double sunk dial, **$100-$200.**

Movement view of Model 306.

Hampden Chronometer, circa 1915, double sunk dial, GF, 21J 16 size, **$295-$400.**

Movement view of the Chronometer.

Hampden William McKinley, circa 1917, 16 size 17J 10k GF, metal dial, **$100-$200.**

Movement view of the William McKinley.

Hampden Dueber, circa 1918, 17J 12 size "Paul Revere" movement, WGF, **$90-$290.**

Case back of the Dueber.

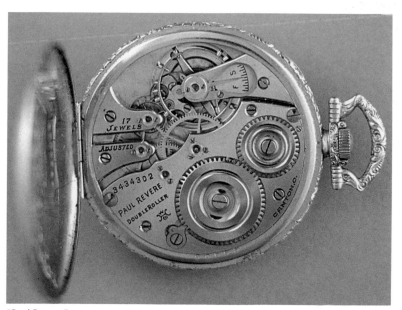

"Paul Revere" movement view.

Dueber Hampden, circa 1918, 12 size 7J, base metal case, **$90-$290.**

Case back of the Dueber.

Hampden "Minuteman," circa 1920, 17J 12 size, white gold-filled case two-tone dial, **$90-$290.**

"Minute Man" movement view.

E. HOWARD & CO.

E. Howard & Co. transition period pendant set, circa 1870s, N size (approx. 18 size), 18k HC, **$1,500-$2,800.**

Edward Howard, a pioneer in American watch history, produced excellent pocket watches at his company in Boston, Mass. Complete watches in their original cases are extremely collectible and sought after. The company was sold to the Keystone Watchcase Co. in 1903. It continued producing fine-quality pocket watches until 1930.

Inside movement view of the watch above.

E. Howard & Co. L size (approx. 16 size), circa 1880s, movement only, **$350.**

Howard-Keystone circa 1910, 21J 16 size, nickel display-type case, **$295-$595.**

Movement view of the watch at left.

Howard circa 1910, GF OF, 17J 12 size, **$100-$200.**

Howard-Keystone Series 11, circa 1913, 21J 16 size, **$395-$795.**

Howard-Keystone circa 1912, RR swing-out case, 21J Series 11 movement, **$395-$795.**

Howard, circa 1915 OF, 16 size 17J WGF, **$195-$295.**

Movement view of the watch at left.

ILLINOIS WATCH CO.

Founded in 1869, this prolific Springfield, Ill., company turned out to be the third-largest producer behind Elgin and Waltham in terms of numbers of jeweled watches produced. In 1927, the company was sold to Hamilton. Its fine quality pocket watches were popular among railroad men, and the line of wristwatches it produced is also highly collectible.

Illinois 17J two-tone checkerboard movement, circa 1896, 18 size, display case, Chalmer pat. Regulator, **$195-$395.**

Movement view of the watch above.

Illinois "The Accurate Time," circa 1898, dial marked Sloan & Feinberg, 18 size, base metal, double sunk dial, **$195-$395.**

Illinois 18 size, circa 1880, silver, very rare floral dial, **$595-$995.**

Illinois Bunn Special, circa 1903, 24J 18 size, movement view, **$1,000-$1,500.**

Inside view of the watch, showing the locomotive on the movement.

Illinois "Locomotive," circa 1887, 11J 18 size KW transition, 4 oz OF silver case, **$295-$595.**

Illinois Sagamo, circa 1902, 23J 16 size, two-tone movement, **$795-$1,295.**

Movement view of the Sagamo.

Illinois Sears and Roebuck Special, circa 1902, 17J 16 size, **$125-$250.**

Movement view of the Sears Special.

Illinois Bunn Special, circa 1904, 24J 18 size, silver swing-out case, **$1,000-$1,500.**

The movement of the Illinois Bunn Special.

A train scene on the case back of the Illinois Bunn Special.

Illinois Burlington Special 16 size, circa 1910, 19J adj., GF, **$150-$350.**

Three-finger bridge movement view of the Burlington Special.

Illinois 17 J, circa 1910, three-finger bridge, **$100-$225.**

Illinois Bunn Special, circa 1923, 23J 16 size, nickel swing-out case, **$600-$1,200.**

Movement view of the Bunn Special.

Illinois Santa Fe Special, circa 1923, 21J 16 size, **$495-$995.**

Movement view of the Santa Fe Special.

Illinois Autocrat, circa 1924, GF, 17J 12 size, **$195-$395.**

Illinois Autocrat movement view.

Illinois Sagamo Special, circa 1925, 23J, solid bow, **$895-$1,395.**

Sagamo Special movement view.

Illinois Bunn Special, 60 hours, circa 1928, WGF, 21J 16 size, **$350-$750.**

Movement view of the Bunn Special.

Illinois Grade 706, circa 1928, 16 size 17J adj. to four positions, WGF, **$195-$395.**

Illinois Bunn Special, Grade 161A, circa 1938, 21J 16 size GF, movement view, **$1,000-$2,000.**

Illinois with fancy GF hunter case, rare fancy dial with butterfly, 16 size, **$595-$995.**

INGERSOLL (ROBERT H. INGERSOLL & BRO.)

Founded in 1881, this New York, N.Y., company produced inexpensive, non-jeweled, "dollar" watches. When competition became fierce among watch companies, Ingersoll sold its watches for $1.

Ingersoll Reliance, circa 1894, 16 size 7J, nickel, **$50-$100.**

Ingersol circa 1890s to 1900s 16 size 7J nickel case, fancy enamel dial, Imperial non magnetic, **$75-$150.**

Movement view of the watch at left.

JAEGER-LECOULTRE

This fine company dates back to 1833, when Antoine LeCoultre established his watchmaking workshop in Le Sentier, Switzerland. In 1847, LeCoultre produced its first movement with a crown winding and setting system, eliminating the need for watch keys. In 1903, the company unveiled the world's flattest pocket watch caliber, and at 1.38 mm thick, it remains an unbroken record.

More history on this company is featured in the section on wristwatches, Pages 189-192.

LeCoultre-Swiss circa 1940s, pocket alarm, brushed aluminum, **$400-$700.**

LONGINES

Founded in 1867, Longines became the world's first watch trademark and the first Swiss company to assemble watches under one roof. In 1877, Longines won the first of its 10 World's Fair grand prizes and 28 gold medals, and it was the beginning of Longines' rightful claim to the title of "The World's Most Honored Watch." In 1899, the Duke of Abbruzi completed a successful Arctic Ocean expedition with Longines chronometers used as instrumentation. In 1927, Colonel Charles Lindbergh completed the first non-stop solo flight from New York to Paris using a Longines watch for time and instrumentation. From 1928 through 1938, the likes of Admiral Byrd, Amelia Earhart, Howard Hughes, Von Schiller (captain of the "Graf Zeppelin"), and other adventurers placed their trust in Longines watches. In 1953, Longines developed the first quartz movement. Stainless steel automatics from the 1950s and 1960s are highly collectible, as are the early Longines wristwatches from the 1910s and 1920s.

The first Longines watch, caliber 840 hand-winding mechanical movement, circa 1867, HC silver pocket watch, white dial inscribed with 12 Roman numerals, sub-seconds at 6 o' clock. *Photo courtesy Longines Museum Collection.*

Longines circa 1878, 11J, nickel,
$95-$295.

Movement view of the watch at left.

Longines-Swiss, circa 1885, HC LS, 800 silver, **$250-$450.**

Longines case front with fob.

Longines J.B. Hudson & Son, circa 1920s, 14k 17J 5 adjustments, **$295-$495.**

Circa 1920 19-ligne minute repeater movement, chronograph, enameled 18k HC with gold dial, Breguet-style numerals. *Photo courtesy Longines Museum Collection.*

Circa 1919 HC set with diamonds, rubies and emeralds, personalized with a monogram, dial enhanced with painted Arabic numerals. *Photo courtesy Longines Museum Collection.*

MOVADO

In 1881, Achille Ditesheim, barely 19 years old and fresh out of watch-making school, founded his own company in Switzerland and was soon joined by three of his brothers. In 1905, a new modern factory was built and a new company name was introduced: Movado. Movado means "always in motion" in the international language of Esperanto.

In the first decade of the 20th century, when the market was still geared to pocket watches, Movado advanced the development of the wristwatch movement. The company was regarded as a pioneer in miniaturized movements and in 1912 introduced the Polyplan watch. The ultimate in conception, design and engineering, Polyplan housed one of the earliest patented "form" movements, constructed on three planes inside a curved case that followed the natural contours of the wrist.

In 1926, the company launched a new watch design called the Ermeto. One of the most unusual watches ever created, this unique pillow-shaped pocket watch housed a patented movement that was wound by the sliding motion of the case as it was opened and closed. The sections of the two-part metal case opened like curtains to reveal the dial. A single opening provided sufficient winding of the mainspring for four hours running time; with six openings, it would run all day and night. The name "Ermeto" was derived from the Greek word meaning "sealed."

View of the Movado factory in La Chaux-de-Fonds, circa 1955.

Although not actually air or water tight, the term suggested protection against shock, dust and temperature changes. Carried loose or attached to a chain, Ermeto was known as the only watch suitable for both men and women—a novel concept at the time. The 1930s were productive years for Movado. The factory developed its two-button Chronograph wristwatches with calendar indications that even included moon phases. Movado began production of wristwatches with automatic winding in 1945, and in 1946 it introduced the Calendomatic. These self-winding wristwatches are still among the most nostalgic collectibles ever produced by Movado.

The next technological advancement in automatic watches came in 1956 with the introduction of the Kingmatic, a series of rotor-driven timepieces.

A prophetic moment for Movado occurred in 1947 when Nathan George Horwitt, an adherent of the Bauhaus design movement and one of America's outstanding designers, set out to simplify the wristwatch. His solution became a legend in modern design known as the Movado Museum Watch. "We do not know time as a number sequence," he said, "but by the position of the sun as the earth rotates." Applying this theory, he eliminated the numerals from the dial. Strongly influenced by the clean, spare lines of the Bauhaus, he designed a dial defined by a single gold dot symbolizing the sun at high noon, the hands suggesting the movement of the earth.

Horwitt's prototype was selected by the Museum of Modern Art in 1960 for its permanent collection. The name, the Museum Watch, is so integral to the company's image that to many it is the first timepiece that comes to mind when they think of Movado.

Movado chronometer, circa 1920s, 18k gold, rare shaped case, **$2,400-$3,000.**

Movado circa 1930s, metal dial, gold applied numbers, **$150-$400.**

Movado circa 1930, Swiss steel case.

Movado Ermeto, circa 1940s, purse watch, small size-leather, **$195-$395.**

Ermeto purse watch closed.

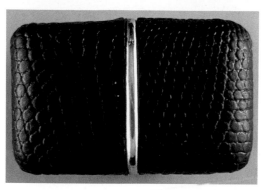

Movado Ermeto Chronometer, circa 1930s, sterling silver gold wash, winds as you open and close the case, **$295-$495.**

Movado Ermeto Chronometer, opening and closing winds movement, black enamel-purse watch, **$295-$495.**

ULYSSE NARDIN

Founded in 1846, this renowned Swiss company is known for its early high-precision marine chronometers. In 1935, Ulysse Nardin developed the caliber 22-24, the first Chronometer with split-second fly-back hands measuring 1/10th of a second. Used at the Berlin Olympic Games in 1936, they earned the company many gold medals and Grand Prix prizes for their accuracy and perfection. This company still produces extremely high-quality watches.

Ulysse Nardin HC chronograph, circa late 1800s, **$1,500-$2,000.** *Photo courtesy of Ulysse Nardin.*

Pocket chronometer-chronograph, made for the Chicago Exhibition of 1893, 18k and silver, **$60,000-$80,000.** *Photo courtesy of Ulysse Nardin.*

Ulysse Nardin-Swiss, circa 1910s, enamel dial radium numbers, silver, **$450-$750.**

Ulysse Nardin split-second chronograph, circa 1890, silver 23J, **$2,500-$3,000.** *Photo courtesy of Antiquorum.*

Ulysse Nardin deck chronometer, circa 1912, sterling, **$1,500-$2,000.** *Photo courtesy of Antiquorum.*

Ulysse Nardin deck chronometer with power reserve indicator, circa 1940, **$3,000-$4,000.** *Photo courtesy of Antiquorum.*

Pocket Watches

NEW HAVEN (NEW HAVEN CLOCK CO.)

This watch company of New Haven, Conn., was in operation from 1853 to 1946.

New Haven pin lever, chrome case dollar watch, **$65-$95.**

Movement view of the watch above.

NEW YORK STANDARD WATCH CO.

The New York Standard Watch Co. was incorporated in 1885 in Jersey City, N.J. The company first produced an 18-size quick train open-faced movement and made its own cases. The first watches were made in 1888. In 1903 the company was sold to the Keystone Case Co. and production continued until 1929.

New York Standard 0 size 7J GP, circa 1900s, enamel dial, pocket or pendant/early wristwatch, **$75-$150.**

New York Standard Watch Co. Perfection U.S.A., circa 1900s-1920s, 7J 16 size, nickel case, two-tone dial, **$95-$150.**

OMEGA

This prolific company from Switzerland first started producing watches in 1848 and is famed for its timing of the Olympics for decades. In 1969, Neil Armstrong stepped onto the lunar surface wearing an Omega Speedmaster Professional, the only watch ever worn on the moon, and to this day the only watch issued to every NASA astronaut. Omega watches are very collectible, especially the "Seamaster" and the "Constellation" automatic models, as well as any of its Chronographs.

Omega circa 1905, 14k multicolored HC fancy dial, 16 size, 21J, **$4,000-$5,000.** *Photo courtesy of Antiquorum.*

Omega case back. *Photo courtesy of Antiquorum.*

Omega 14k OF, rare dial, **$495-$895.**

Omega 15J, circa 1930s, unusual stainless case, **$250-$450.**

Omega-Swiss circa 1974, stainless steel, hacking feature, **$195-$395.**

Movement view of the watch at left.

PATEK PHILIPPE

Founded in 1839 and considered to be one of the most important watchmakers in the world, this high-end company from Switzerland produced, and still creates, incredible works of art.

These watches are built to last and have been purchased throughout the company's 160-plus-year history by notables such as Queen Victoria, Rudyard Kipling, Albert Einstein, Leo Tolstoy, and Marie Curie. Every Patek is collectible.

Patek Philippe, A.H. Rodanet & Co. Paris, circa 1870s, 18k, Roman numerals, **$2,000-$3,000.**

Patek Philippe Shreve & Co., San Francisco, circa 1882, chronograph 18k HC photo on dial, 21J, **$5,000-$6,000.** *Photo courtesy of Antiquorum.*

Patek Philippe Bailey Banks & Biddle, minute repeater with split-second chronograph, circa 1913, 18k 40J 8 adjustments, **$18,000-$22,000.** *Photo courtesy of Antiquorum.*

Patek Philippe Shreve & Co., circa 1896, 18k pink gold case, unusual sweep second, **$2,500-$3,500.**

Movement view of the Patek Philippe.

Patek Philippe & Cie, circa 1920s, 18k, 18J-gold metal dial, **$2,000-$3,000.**

Patek Philippe & Cie, presentation watch, circa 1920s, 18k, 18J, **$2,000-$3,000.**

Movement view of the 18J watch.

Movement view of the 18J 8.

Patek Philippe R. J. Richards Co., Massachusetts, circa 1920s, 18k, 18J 8 adj., **$2,000-$3,000.**

Movement view of the 12 Ligne.

Patek Philippe ladies pendant monogrammed case, circa 1900, 12 Ligne 18k HC, **$1,800-$2,500.**

ROCKFORD WATCH CO.

Rockford Watch Co. silver HC, circa 1870s, 18 size, key wind key set, **$295-$495.**

This Rockford, Ill., company, in operation from 1874-1915, produced a small number of high-grade watches. The highest grades of the early Rockford watches are engraved "Ruby Jewels" or "Ruby." Later this became a stylized letter "R" associated with the jewel count.

The company also had a major focus on the railroad watch industry and many watches are labeled "RG" for Railroad Grade.

Rockford Watch Co. 18 size KW transition, circa 1880s, rare 24-hour dial, **$1,200-$1,700.**

Rockford Watch Co. 18 size 11J lever set, circa 1882, sub seconds at 3 o'clock, 14k, **$1,200-$1,700.** *Photo courtesy of Antiquorum.*

Rockford Watch Co. 15J 18 size, circa 1886, GF fancy engraved HC, **$195-$395.**

Rockford Watch Co. 18 size 16J GF, circa 1899, fancy dial, **$1,200-$1,500.** *Photo courtesy of Antiquorum.*

Rockford Watch Co. 16 size 15J, circa 1900, very rare aluminum movement, in nickel display case, est. **$6,500-$8,500.** *Photo courtesy of Antiquorum.*

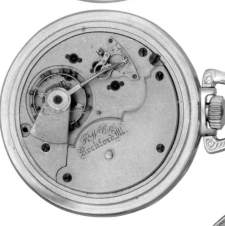

Movement of the rare aluminum watch. *Photo courtesy of Antiquorum.*

Rockford Watch Co. 16 size 15J, circa 1904, unusual red dial, **$2,000-$2,500.** *Photo courtesy of Antiquorum.*

AUTHORITIES are agreed that THE ROCKFORD is the best American-made watch. The watch of Quality —Efficiency. The choice of those who insist upon mechanical perfection. The manufacturers of the ROCKFORD WATCH co-operate with the legitimate retail jeweler to the fullest extent. They have eliminated the jobber and sell only direct to the retail jeweler. The ROCKFORD Watch Company neither sell nor manufacture under their own name or any other name for Mail Order, Catalog Houses or Department Stores

Rockford Watch Co.
ROCKFORD
ILLINOIS

Rockford watch ad.

SOUTH BEND WATCH CO.

In 1903, three brothers, George, Clement and John M. Studebaker, bought the Columbus Watch Co., moved it to South Bend, Ind., and changed the name to South Bend Watch Co. The company produced watches in the style of the Columbus Watch Co. and its movements were identified as model 1, 2, or 3, with grades numbering 100 to 431. Even-number grades denoted hunting-case movements, while odd-number grades were for open-face cases. The company was in operation until 1929.

South Bend Grade 227 RR, circa 1928, 21J 16 size, double sunk dial, **$250-$500**.

Watch movement of the Grade 227 shown above.

South Bend Watch Co. OF Montgomery dial RR, **$250-$500**.

South Bend Watch Co. Studebaker, circa 1927, 21J 12 size, GF, **$200-$400.**

Movement view of the Studebaker piece.

South Bend Watch Co. model 429, circa 1928, OF 12 size, **$100-$200.**

VACHERON CONSTANTIN

One of the oldest Swiss watch companies, dating back to the 1700s, Vacheron Constantin has created some of the most beautiful watches the world has ever seen.

It ranks among the top makers and is still in existence today. Its high-quality timepieces are extremely collectible and valuable.

Vacheron Constantin-Swiss, circa 1870s, 18k fancy engraved HC, **$1,750-$2,500.**

The fancy engraved case of the watch above.

Vacheron Constantin-Swiss presentation watch, circa 1949, rare aluminum case, **$1,500-$2,500.**

The inscribed case of the presentation watch.

Vacheron Constantin deck chronometer, circa 1955, power reserve indicator, silver, **$3,500-$4,500.** *Photo courtesy of Antiquorum.*

WALTHAM WATCH CO. (AMERICAN WALTHAM WATCH CO.)

This is the granddaddy of large American watch companies. Its beginnings were in the early 1850s in Waltham, Mass., and it produced high-quality watches of every grade. Early examples of Waltham timepieces are valuable collectors' items and highly sought after.

This company was always innovative and the pioneering spirit of the people who worked at Waltham spawned the development of the watch industry in this country.

Waltham Model 1883, circa 1888, GF OF 18 size, fancy dial, bird scene, **$400-$700.**

Waltham 11J 18 size, circa 1884, 14k Elk motif box hinge HC, **$1,000-$2,000.**

Elk motif on the case.

Waltham 14 size, circa 1885, GF HC, fancy pink and green floral dial, **$250-$700.**

Waltham LS, 6 size, circa 1885, 11J OF, 14k, **$150-$275.**

Waltham Model 1883, circa 1887, 18 size Appleton Tracy movement, nickel display case, **$125-$250.**

Appleton Tracy movement view.

Waltham 6 size LS 7J, circa 1887, 14k, **$250-$400.**

Case front view.

Case back.

Inside movement view.

Canadian Pacific Railway movement view, showing the beaver logo.

Waltham Model 1883, Canadian Pacific Railway, circa 1888, 17J 18 size, **$500-$1,000.**

Crescent St. movement view.

Waltham Crescent St., circa 1888, model 1883, 18 size 15J, nickel swing-out case, **$195-$295.**

Waltham 2/0 size, circa 1889, set with 76 diamonds on front and rear, enamel portrait hand painted on case back, high grade movement, **$3,500-$5,000.**

The enamel portrait painted on the back of the case.

The 2/0 size high grade movement.

Waltham 15J GF, circa 1891, fancy dial with blue inner chapters and red dots, 6 size HC, **$195-$395.**

American Waltham 18 size, circa 1890s, nickel case, fancy dial, **$250-$550.**

Waltham OF, 14k, 0 size, circa 1891, fancy dial, **$795-$995.**

Case back view.

Waltham "Santa Fe Route," circa 1892, 17J 18 size, **$595-$1,195.**

Santa Fe Route movement view.

American Waltham OF, GF, 6 size, circa 1894, fancy dial, **$150-$225.**

Waltham Riverside Maximus, circa 1901, 23J 16 size PS, **$495-$995.**

Inside view of Riverside movement.

Waltham Vanguard, circa 1902, 19J 16 size, double sunk dial, **$150-$350.**

Inside view of Vanguard movement.

Waltham Vanguard movement view, circa 1903, 19J 18 size, **$175-$400.**

Waltham 18 size, 21J grade, 845 RR, circa 1904, base metal, **$295-$495.**

Movement view of the 845 21J.

Case back of the 845 21J RR.

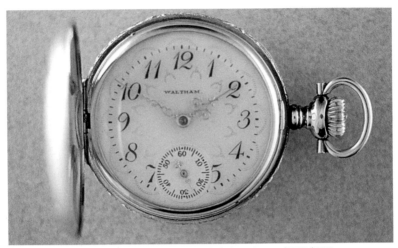

Waltham 14k HC, circa 1905, gold and enamel dial, 7J O size, **$495-$795.**

The fancy case of the watch above.

Waltham "Maximus," circa 1910, gold case, **$1,100.**

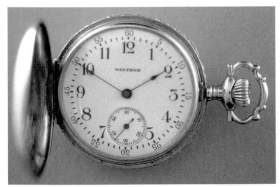

Waltham 15J, circa 1912, 14k HC, O size, **$250-$400.**

Front view of the case.

The case back.

Inside movement view.

Waltham Opera watch, circa 1912 GF, approximately 16 size case, 0 size movement, **$150-$250.**

Waltham 16 size 17J lever set, circa 1913, nickel swing-out case, **$150-$225.**

Movement view of the 17J.

Waltham Crescent St., circa 1919, GF, 16 size, model 1908, 21J metal dial, **$295-$495.**

Crescent St. movement view.

Waltham Equity, circa 1920, 16 size GF 15J, **$100-$150.**

Waltham 17J 12 size, circa 1920, WGF case, metal dial, **$125-$225.**

Waltham 17J 12 size, circa 1923, 14k white/personalized dial, **$195-$395.**

Waltham Vanguard with up-down indicator, circa 1926, 23J RR, **$600-$1,100.**

Movement view of the 23J.

Waltham Vanguard with up-down indicator, GF 16 size, double sunk, bold dial, **$695-$1,295.**

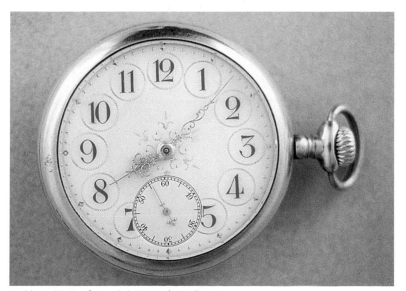

Waltham 16 size, fancy dial, GF OF, **$250-$350.**

WATERBURY WATCH CO.

This company of Waterbury, Conn., started producing inexpensive watches in 1880 for those who couldn't afford the more expensive pieces made by Elgin, Waltham and other companies. Waterbury had great success initially, but because so many of the inexpensive watches were given away as premiums with men's and boy's suits, the public came to see the watches as cheap merchandise and sales eventually dwindled. The company later reorganized as the New England Watch Co.

Waterbury Watch Co. Addison Series N, circa 1890s, duplex escapement, silver case, **$75-$95.**

Addison movement view.

Waterbury Watch Co. Addison, GF series N, 0 size, fancy dial and hands, **$95-$195.**

Waterbury Watch Co. 0 size, Duplex movement, silver case, blue blister-type enamel dial, **$95-$195.**

Case back view, with engraving.

Waterbury Watch Co. Addison, series K, Duplex escapement, 18 size, GF, **$95-$195.**

NIELLO POCKET WATCHES - Circa 1900s-1920s

Niello is a form of black enamel decoration used mostly on silver watch cases.
The designs are deeply engraved into
the metal, then filled with the enamel
mixture and heated. The silver, or gold-
inlay high spots, reveal the design. Ni-
ello-type cases were used by many fine
watch companies such as Rolex, Eterna,
and Omega. Depending on the condition, as niello is semi-hard and fragile,
and whether it is a well-known watch
brand, values are $250-$1,200 and up.
The following are just some examples of
Niello.

Niello case with car race scene.

Demi-hunter front.

Demi-hunter back.

Eterna.

Eterna checkerboard case back.

Two women talking.

Bird on branch.

Hunting scene on horseback.

Oriental beauty with elaborate gold head ornament.

Hunter case front-Lion.

Case back-Leopard.

Floral design.

Art Nouveau design.

Another floral design.

Sunburst design.

Fancy two-tone case with emblem.

Flowers with plate for engraving monogram.

Fancy scroll design.

Woman with hair ornament, crackle background.

REPOUSSÉ WATCHES

Repoussé is a style of metalwork where the metal is hammered up from the reverse side to form a design. Depending on the subject portrayed, condition, and size of the case, these artful watches vary in price from $200 to $500 and up. The following are just some examples of repoussé pieces.

French, circa early 1900s, sterling-dragon scene.

Art Nouveau, woman, bird, and four-leaf clover.

Unusual shaped case, floral design.

Unusual shape case, back view.

Three dogs on case.

Ducks and dogs.

Case back, with pointer.

Silver repoussé case, poppy design.

MISCELLANEOUS POCKET WATCHES

Swiss made for English, H. Samuel Manchester, "Acme Lever," 17 ligne silver KW KS, **$200-$350.**

Movement view, key wind key set.

S. Smith & Son 9 Strand, Watchmakers to the Admiralty London, Swiss non-magnetizable, **$150-$300.**

Remontoir 50mm 15 rubis, circa 1890s, Swiss silver massive case, **$295-$495.**

Swiss 10J pin-set cylinder, late 1800s, silver case with fancy dial, **$95-$195.**

Inside Remontoir dust cover view.

Swiss Besancon, La Reine des Montres, cylinder movement, GF 24-hour inner chapter, **$95-$195.**

Swiss watch and timer, start-stop sweep second, silver oversize, **$195-$295.**

Swiss watch/timer back view.

Audemars Freves, Brassus & Geneve, 45mm 14k hunter case, **$695-$895.**

Kienzle Selecta, made in Germany, 17J shockproof chrome case, **$150-$250.**

J. W. Allen, 37 Strand London, circa 1875, oversize Swiss movement, PS, **$250-$450.**

Swiss Frenia, hand-painted blister-type metal dial pin, lever pin set, GP case, **$75-$175.**

Swiss Pearlham, cylinder movement, enamel blister type dial, base metal case, **$95-$150.**

Swiss silver, fancy dial flower in center, 18 ligne pin set, Roman numerals, **$95-$195.**

Swiss silver case back.

Swiss Faro, silver cased pin set, blister metal dial, **$95-$195.**

Back view of Faro engraved case.

Fancy engraved movement.

Swiss Precaution, gun metal with enamel work on back, pin lever pin set, **$100-$200.**

Back view of the Philippine crest of the watch above.

Swiss Pin Set, flowers in center of enamel dial, nickel cased, **$150-$250.**

Engraved scene on back with Swiss cross.

Swiss Systeme Roskopf, pin lever pin set, 19 ligne base metal case, very fancy flower dial, **$100-$200.**

Swiss Roskopf, Cuervo y sobrinos Habana, nickel pin set, **$95-$195.**

Swiss, 18k engraved case, fancy gold colored engraved dial, 13 ligne pin set cylinder movement, **$175-$275.**

Swiss, 18 ligne, white and cobalt blue blister dial, gun metal, fancy gold hands, **$95-$150.**

Swiss silver and gold, heart-shaped cut out dial with flowers, pin set 10J cylinder movement, note: missing hands, **$125-$225.**

The International Watch Co., Jersey City, N.J., Roulette Wheel in PW case, circa 1902, 18 size, nickel plated, **$150-$250.**

CF Greenwood & Bros., Norfolk, VA, very high grade Swiss movement, wolf tooth winding, 11.5 ligne 18k, **$295-$495.**

Movement view of Greenwood & Bros.

Swiss Depose, HC nickel pin set, Brail, blind man's watch, raised brail bumps at hours, heavy duty screwed-on hands, **$150-$250.**

Hunter case PW, collapsing shot glass inside case, approx. 18 size base, **$75-$150.**

PW metal shot glass opened.

Swiss Stratford, Langendorf movement, circa 1920s, 6J, GF, **$75-$175.**

Unusual enamel and gold dial, gun metal case, **$95-$195.**

Swiss, circa 1910s, eight day, visible balance, nickel silver, **$150-$250.**

Swiss eight-day movement.

Girard Perregaux, the Golden Bridge, circa 1890, minute repeater with split-second chronograph, 18k 32J, **$10,000-$12,000.** *Photo courtesy of Antiquorum.*

Gold Bridges movement. *Photo courtesy of Antiquorum.*

Swiss by Tavannes, Chronometre, circa 1900, 17J, sterling with equestrian scene of horse, **$1,650-$2,000.**

Enamel equestrian case back view.

Unusual Swiss, exposed movement, circa 1930s, **$300-$400.**

Swiss Minute Repeater, circa 1890s, 18k gold HC, **$3,500-$5,500.**

Swiss Volta, 1/4 hour repeater, push piece to activate, silver cased, **$1,500-$2,000.**

Back view of high relief repoussé case.

Swiss, 14k gold HC,
$700-$1,200.

Tiffany & Co., five-minute
repeater, circa 1900, 18k,
$6,000-$7,000.

Repeater movement view of the Tiffany
watch.

Front cover view of the Tiffany watch.

Cartier, circa 1915, platinum, diamonds, rock crystal, **$10,000-$12,000.** *Photo courtesy of Antiquorum.*

Cartier, Montre Bousolle Cadran Solaire, dress watch compass and sundial, circa 1938, 18k, **$4,000-$5,000.** *Photo courtesy of Antiquorum.*

Rolex, purse watch Sporting Princess Chronometre, circa 1936, **$3,500-$4,500.** *Photo courtesy of Antiquorum.*

Swiss purse watch, enamel on silver case with pink roses, Art Deco, **$195-$395.**

Wristwatches

In the early years, wristwatches, also called "wristlets," were thought to be something to be worn by a lady; men were only interested in carrying pocket watches. The market for men's wristwatches changed after soldiers began wearing them during combat and by World War I, wristwatches were in high demand by soldiers. Vintage military watches are highly coveted by collectors today.

There have been many more changes to the standard wristwatch through the years and it has become more than something that tells time. With more complex movements come alarms, day and date of the week information, water resistance and some even offer the phases of the moon. What once was something you had to manually wind eventually became self-winding, electric, quartz and also LCD.

Collecting wristwatches has become quite the phenomenon and you can find something to fit any price range.

The following watches are just a small sampling of timepieces waiting to be discovered. Watches are listed alphabetically by maker.

Alpha 18k pink with black dial, circa late 1940s early 1950s, large teardrop lugs, **$500-$700.**

Audemars Piguet 18k, circa 1968, **$3,500-$4,500.** *Photo courtesy of Antiquorum.*

BENRUS WATCH CO.

An American company, Benrus was founded in New York City in the 1920s by brothers Benjamin and Russel Lazrus; the name comes from the first three letters in Benjamin and the last three in Lazrus.

During World War II, the company produced moderately priced wristwatches and the designs it created after the war are noted for their stylish and fancy lugs, bezels and dials.

In the 1950s, Benrus was one of the top three watch companies in the U.S., along with Hamilton and Bulova.

Benrus GF stainless back, circa late 1930s early 1940s, 17J, **$75-$125.**

Benrus square two-tone, circa 1920s-30s, chrome with gold bezel, 15J, **$95-$195.**

Benrus GF case, circa 1940s, sub-seconds/ large lugs, **$95-$195.**

Benrus with day date, circa late 1940s, GF stainless back, 17J, **$95-$195.**

Benrus manual wind, rotating bezel, stainless, **$75-$150.**

Benrus 21J GF, circa 1950s, fancy lugs, **$100-$200.**

BLANCPAIN

Since 1735, Blancpain of Switzerland, the world's oldest watch brand, has symbolized the finest in traditional mechanical watch making. Through its famous slogan, "Since 1735, there has never been a quartz Blancpain watch, and there never will be," the brand has consistently made clear its determination to perpetuate this remarkable know-how, the pride of Swiss watch making.

In 1926, Blancpain contributed to watch history by producing the prototype of the first wristwatch with an "automatic" wind mechanism, for the famous "Harwood," the invention of English horologist John Harwood. In 1953, Blancpain released the "Fifty Fathoms." Water-resistant to 50 fathoms (300 feet), it would soon become a precious tool for divers the world over. Jacques Cousteau and his divers wore this watch when they made the film, "The World of Silence," in 1956, and it was soon recognized and adopted by the armed forces of several nations, including the U.S. Navy and the French and German armies. This famous firm still produces mechanical watches to this day and is regarded as one of the top makers.

Blancpain Fifty Fathoms divers' watches, stainless steel-automatic, circa 1950s, **$1,500-$3,000.**

BREITLING

This Swiss company was founded in 1884 by Leon Breitling. It first specialized in producing chronograph pocket watches and introduced the first wristwatch chronograph in 1915 for pilots in World War I. The company had strong ties to aviation and is known for developing a watch with a second return-to-zero pushpiece and launching the Chronomat, the first chronograph to be fitted with a circular slide rule.

In 1952, the company also created the Navitimer, a wrist instrument equipped with the famous "navigation computer" that could handle all calculations for a flight plan. The company continues to produce high-quality watches.

Breitling Geneve Navitimer, chronograph, circa 1960s, black dial, white bezel, **$1,200-$1,600.**

Breitling Datora chronograph, circa 1952, SS triple date, **$1,600-$2,000.** *Photo courtesy of Antiquorum.*

Breitling Chronograph, circa 1940s, triple date, 18k pink, **$1,000-$2,000.** *Photo courtesy of Antiquorum.*

Breitling Navitimer model 806, circa 1967, three register, stainless, **$1,000-$1,800.**

Breitling chronograph three register, stainless, **$900-$1,100.**

Breitling Navitimer, rare date model timer lower right corner, stainless, **$1,500-$2,500.**

Breitling Chronomat, chronograph automatic, circa 1970s, SS, **$700-$900.** *Photo courtesy of Antiquorum.*

Breitling Navitimer Chrono-matic, circa 1970s, SS black dial, **$800-$1,000.** *Photo courtesy of Antiquorum.*

Breitling Chronometre, "Navitimer," 2006, **$3,200.**

BULOVA

This highly successful American watch company is noted for its Art Deco wristwatches of the 1920s and 1930s, and for the huge success of its "Accutron" tuning-fork watch, produced well into the 1970s.

Bulova ladies, circa 1920s, unusual 19k engraved case, engraved sterling silver dial, **$100-$250.**

Ladies case back.

A small Bulova watch movement.

Bulova with chrome stepped case, circa 1920s, radium hands with sub-seconds, **$75-$175.**

Design on the back.

Bulova ladies, rare blue enamel and 14k bow design, ribbon band, **$495-$795.**

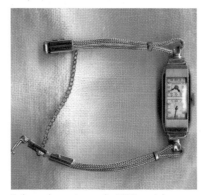

Bulova doctor's watch, 1920, stainless steel, **$250.**

Bulova with chrome tank case and engraved bezel, circa 1930s, sub-seconds, **$95-$195.**

Bulova gold filled, unusual case, circa 1939, two-tone black and gray dial, **$200-$400.**

Bulova with diamonds, circa 1940s, 23J, 14k WG, **$195-$395.**

Bulova with WGF case, circa 1950s, hidden lugs, **$75-$175.**

Restored Bulova, circa 1950s, gold filled diamond dial, after dial restoration, **$95-$195.**

Bulova 17J, circa 1959, self winding, GF with black dial, **$95-$195.**

Bulova with triangular case, circa 1960, 23J GP, stainless back, **$495-$695.**

Bulova GF, circa 1966, 30J, self winding, unusual date window at 4:00, **$100-$250.**

Bulova Accutron 214, circa 1966 (M6), GF, **$175-$275.**

Bulova Accutron 214, circa 1967 (M7), stainless/unusual lugs, **$200-$400.**

Bulova Spaceview, Accutron model 214, circa 1971, see-through crystal case, stainless, **$250-$395.**

Bulova digital LED, 1970s, gold tone, **$150-$300.**

Bulova ladies retro, stainless, 1970s, **$50.**

Bulova Accutron Model 218, circa 1973, stainless, **$125-$225.**

Bulova Accutron Model 214, circa 1974, railroad approved, **$395-$495.**

Bulova 214 Accutron Anniversary Edition, gold-plate case, stainless back, designed in the shape of the Accutron tuning fork, Spaceview, **$395-$595.**

Bulova Accutron railroad approved wristwatch, **$100-$125.**

Bulova Accutron railroad approved wristwatch, **$100-$150.**

Bulova Accutron wristwatch, **$10-$20.**

Bulova Accutron wristwatch, **$20-$30.**

Bulova ladies Accutron quartz wristwatch N9, **$18-$25.**

Bulova ladies wristwatch, **$125-$175.**

Bulova calendar wristwatch, **$20-$25.**

Bulova Accutron date wristwatch #2181, **$40-$50.**

Bulova self-winding wristwatch, **$70-$90.**

Bulova 10 An 21J disc second wristwatch, **$100-$130.**

Bulova wristwatch, **$20-$25.**

Bulova nurse's watch, chrome plated, 1930s, **$300.**

Bulova Accutron N5 wristwatch, **$40-$50.**

Bulova railroad approved Accutron wristwatch, **$70-$90.**

ELGIN NATIONAL WATCH CO.

Founded in 1864, this Elgin, Ill., company produced more jeweled watches than any other in America during its more than 90-year history. The company made low-end watches, all the way up through to its famous high-quality railroad grades. The company's Art Deco wristwatches are highly collectible. Some of the company's pocket watches are shown on Pages 32-49.

Elgin engraved bezel style/base metal, circa 1910s, enamel dial blue spade hands, 15J, **$95-$195.**

Inside view of the watch at left.

Montgomery Bros. Elgin 15J movement, circa 1911, sterling-enamel dial, **$195-$495.**

Elgin 15J, circa 1915, chrome engraved, radium hands and numerals, **$95-$195.**

Elgin military, circa 1917, nickel case, 7J, heavy wire lugs-radium hands, **$150-$450.**

Elgin with enamel dial, circa 1918, silver, wire lug, **$150-$350.**

Elgin 7J, circa 1918, watch band pins riveted on, GF, **$100-$250.**

Inside movement view of the watch at left.

Elgin 7J, circa 1920s, enamel dial with sub seconds, GF swivel lugs, **$95-$195.**

Elgin 7J, circa 1920s?, GF, rare case style, **$150-$300.**

Elgin 15J, circa 1922, WGF case, engraved bezel edge, **$95-$195.**

Elgin 14k WG with barrel-shaped case, circa 1927, large crown, 15J, **$75-$150.**

Elgin military, sterling silver, 1920s, **$225.**

Elgin 7J, circa 1929, WGF case, engraved bezel, **$75-$175.**

Elgin GF stepped case, circa 1930s, **$95-$225.**

Ladies Elgin, 1930s, **$150.**

Elgin Avigo, circa 1930s, 7J, chrome case, **$100-$250.**

Elgin 7J, circa 1932, WGF engraved square case, **$100-$250.**

Elgin with curved case, circa 1933, hidden lugs, 7J, chrome case unusual design, **$100-$300.**

Elgin mid-size, circa 1939, 15J, sweep second hand, **$75-$150.**

Elgin movement and inside case back of the watch at top right.

Lord Elgin, driver's style black dial, circa 1950s, 21J, GF, **$100-$250.**

Elgin step-case, 1940s, **$125.**

Elgin driver's watch, pink dial, circa 1950s, 21J, pink GF, **$100-$250.**

Lord Elgin 21J, GF, circa 1951, **$75-$175.**

Lord Elgin, movement caliber 670.

Lord Elgin gold filled, circa 1950s, fancy hidden lugs, **$95-$195.**

Lord Elgin GF square case, circa 1950s, 21J, **$95-$195.**

Elgin with pinwheel dial, circa 1950s, numerals on bezel, GF, **$95-$195.**

Elgin 18k gold, made to commemorate 50 millionth watch, gold-plated movement, numbered edition of 1,000, 1951, **$1,600.**

Elgin 17J, GF, circa 1952, **$75-$175.**

Lord Elgin digital, circa 1950s, 21J caliber movement, GF, **$400-$800.**

Lord Elgin direct read-with box, circa 1950s, GF, **$495-$695.**

Elgin sportsman wristwatch, **$60-$80.**

Elgin money clip, circa 1950s, 17J, GF, **$95-$295.**

Lord Elgin 559 21J 14k wristwatch, **$100-$150.**

Elgin Swissonic wristwatch, **$25-$35.**

Elgin Liberty Head coins wristwatch, **$90-$120.**

GIRARD-PERREGAUX

Founded in the 1850s, this Swiss company is the first to produce wristwatches (1880s) for military use.

Girard-Perregaux "Sea Hawk," circa late 1940s, stainless, two-tone dial, **$195-$395.**

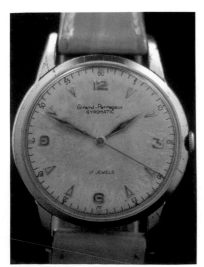

Girard-Perregaux Gyromatic, chrome plated, 17J, **$95-$195.**

Girard-Perregaux Gyromatic, circa late 1950s-1960s, SS back/gold top/original dial, screw back, **$100-$250.**

Girard-Perregaux 101-226 14k gold
wristwatch, **$275-$325.**

Girard-Perregaux automatic wristwatch,
$90-$110.

Girard-Perregaux
GXM 14k wristwatch,
$50-$60.

Girard-Perregaux wrist-
watch, **$100-$150.**

Girard Perregaux
ladies wristwatch,
$75-$125.

GRUEN WATCH CO.

Founded in the 1870s in Cincinnati, Ohio, Gruen is famous for its imported Swiss "Guild" movements, and for the "Veri-Thin," "Curvex" and "Doctors" watches. Some of the company's pocket watches are shown on Pages 50-52.

Gruen Precision ladies, circa 1920s, 14k WG, diamond, **$395-$795.**

Gruen 17J, circa 1930s, GF barrel shape, **$95-$195.**

Gruen Swiss, circa 1930, 15J, GF stepped case, **$95-$195.**

Gruen Model 700, circa 1930s, 10k GF, 15J, restored dial, **$125.**

Gruen ladies Curvex, circa 1930s, GF, **$100-$250.**

Group of ladies Gruen wristwatches, circa 1930s, 1940s and 1950s, **$50-$100.**

Gruen Curvex Precision, circa 1940s, GF hooded lugs, 17J, **$195-$395.**

Gruen Veri-Thin, circa 1940s, 24-hour military dial radium hands, GF, **$100-$250.**

Gruen Veri-Thin Precision, circa 1940s, 14k, doctor's watch, **$795-$995.**

Gruen Veri-Thin, circa 1945, 10k, GF, stainless back, 15J, **$95-$195.**

Gruen Veri-Thin, circa 1940s-1950s, GF fancy rectangle case, **$100-$250.**

Gruen Precision, circa 1950s, auto wind/ sweep second, GF, **$75-$175.**

Gruen Precision-auto wind, circa 1960s, day date, SS, **$75-$175.**

Ladies Gruen precision 275 17J 14k wristwatch, **$50-$60.**

Gruen Precision electronic wristwatch, **$25-$35.**

Gruen 14k yellow gold, diamond dial, 1950s, **$650**.

Gruen Veri-Thin with flip-up lid, yellow gold filled, circa 1950, **$800.**

Gruen center sweep, pink gold filled, sterling silver back, 1940s, **$300**.

Gruen see-through, auto-wind, stainless steel, circa 1951, **$250**.

Gruen Veri-Thin, pink gold filled, stainless steel-back, 1940s, **$300**.

Gruen Veri-Thin, center sweep, yellow gold filled, stainless steel back, 1940s, **$400**.

Gruen Veri-Thin, center sweep, yellow gold filled, stainless steel back, 1940s, **$300**.

Gruen Curvex, side wrist, yellow gold filled, late 1940s, **$1,000**.

Gruen "mystery watch," auto-wind, 14k yellow gold, circa 1950, **$500**.

Gruen one-button Chrono-Timer, 14k yellow gold, 1946, **$1,800**.

Gruen "mystery watch," auto-wind, 14k yellow gold filled, circa 1950, **$225**.

Gruen alarm, yellow gold filled, 1950s, **$250**.

Gruen diver's watch, stainless steel, 1950s, **$200**.

Gruen auto-wind with "up-down indicator," shows hours of operation remaining, yellow gold filled, 1950s, **$250**.

Gruen diver's watch, stainless steel, circa 1960, **$150**.

Gruen diver's watch with pop-out movement, radium numbers (flaking), sterling silver, 1915, **$500**.

Gruen Carré, 14k gold, red and black enamel, 1930s, **$3,500**.

Gruen Carré, chrome plated, black and red paint, 1930s, **$450**.

Gruen Carré, yellow gold filled, 1930s, **$500**.

Gruen Carré, base metal case, would have been leather covered, 1930s, **$250**.

Gruen Curvex, 41mm, platinum, 1940s, **$3,500**.

Gruen Curvex, 47mm, yellow gold filled, 1940s, **$600**.

Gruen Curvex, 42 mm, yellow gold filled, 1940s, **$275**.

Gruen Curvex, 45mm, gold filled, 1940s, **$400**.

Ladies Gruen Curvex, pink gold filled, 1940s, with Madonna tag, **$100.**

Ladies Gruen Curvex, side wrist, gold filled, 1940s, **$300**.

Gruen 14k gold with band, 1920s, 24mm, **$600**.

Gruen ladies Curvex, 38mm, pink gold filled, 1940s, **$150**.

Curvex 1940s ladies, yellow gold filled, **$75-$110**.

Gruen nurse's watch, 14k gold, band gold filled, 1920s, **$200**.

HAMILTON WATCH CO.

Hamilton 17J 986 caliber, circa 1930s, rare sub seconds at 9:00, GF/early refinished dial, **$200-$300.**

Founded in 1892, this Lancaster, Pa., company is regarded by many collectors as the premier watch manufacturer in American history. The company produced high-quality watches and was popular in the railroad industry. The master watchmaker I worked for in the 1970s timed every watch that left the store using a Hamilton 992B pocket watch that hung on a nail in the repair room.

Hamilton made watch-making history when it introduced its battery-powered wristwatch in 1957. Hamilton railroad pocket watches are sought after by collectors, as are examples from the large wristwatch line that it produced. Some of the company's pocket watches are shown on Pages 53-62.

Hamilton 987A movement, circa 1930s, barrel shape, 17J, **$100-$200.**

Hamilton Piping Rock, circa 1928, 14k white or yellow, enamel bezel, **$800-$1,400.**

Hamilton square dial, circa 1923, green GF-enameled bezel, sub-seconds at 9:00, rare. Price not determined.

Hamilton Coronado, circa 1930s, 14k WG swivel lugs, black enamel bezel, **$1,000-$2,400.**

Hamilton "Dixon," circa 1936, stepped lugs, applied numerals, 17J 987E movement, GF, **$100-$250.**

Hamilton Seckron, circa 1936, GF, doctor's watch, **$800-$1,300.**

Hamilton Rutledge, circa 1936, platinum, **$1,200-$2,500.**

Hamilton Gilman, circa 1937, 14k, **$350-$700.**

Hamilton "Brock," circa 1939, Grade 982, 14k, 19J, **$395-$795.**

Hamilton Dodson, circa 1937, 17J, GF, **$100-$275.**

Hamilton Sidney, circa 1937, GF, **$100-$300.**

Hamilton WGF, circa 1940s, 17J 752 movement, applied numerals, **$100-$250.**

Hamilton "Martin," circa 1941, 987A movement, GF, **$100-$200.**

Hamilton military WW II, new-old stock, **$300-$400.**

Hamilton Automatic, circa 1950, **$125.**

Hamilton "Assymetic" electric, 1950s, **$450.**

Hamilton "Assymetic" electric, 1950s, **$350.**

Hamilton Transcontinental A, circa 1955, GF/time-zone dial, **$300-$750.**

Hamilton Van Horn Electric, circa 1957, 14k, **$300-$500.**

Hamilton Ventura Electric, circa 1957, 14k yellow, **$1,200-$1,800.**

Hamilton Victor Electric, circa 1957, GF, **$125-$375.**

Hamilton Ventura Electric, circa 1958, 14k white diamond dial, **$3,000-$5,000.**

Hamilton Pacer Electric, circa 1958, GF, **$350-$850.**

Hamilton Pacer Electric, circa late 1950s, corporate logo dial, **$300-$700.**

Hamilton Ventura Electric, late 1950s, 18k pink gold, very rare. No established value.

Hamilton "Prentice," circa 1959, RGF, author's gold and rosewood band attached, $95-$195.

Hamilton Regulus Electric, circa 1959, SS, $400-$900.

Hamilton Saturn Electric, circa 1960, GF, $350-$650.

Hamilton "Thin-O-Matic" (rare), automatic, circa 1960, two-tone dial, GF, $395-$695.

Hamilton Altair Electric, circa 1962, GF, original band, $1,800-$3,000.

Hamilton Savitar Electric, circa 1962, 14k, **$400-$900.**

Hamilton Taurus Electric, circa 1962, GF, **$100-$350.**

Hamilton Vega Electric, circa 1962, GF, original band, **$800-$1,500.**

Hamilton Victor II Electric, circa 1962, GF, original band, **$200-$500.**

Hamilton RR special electric, circa 1963, 505 model, stainless, **$175-$275.**

Hamilton Polaris Electric, circa 1963, 14k, **$395-$595.**

Hamilton Savitar II Electric, circa 1965, General Electric corporate logo, **$200-$500.**

Hamilton T-403 Automatic, two-tone dial with date, circa 1965, GF, **$395-$695.**

Hamilton Lord Lancaster J Electric, circa 1965, GF/diamond dial, **$300-$700.**

Hamilton electric, 1960s, **$350.**

Hamilton Odyssee 2001 Automatic, circa 1969, date at 6:00, SS, **$500-$900.**

Hamilton black dial wristwatch, **$60-$70.**

Hamilton Vesta, ladies version of the Altair, original box, GF, **$300-$700.**

Hamilton wristwatch, **$200-$250.**

Hamilton 757 14k ladies wristwatch, **$40-$50.**

Hamilton ladies wrist-watch, **$450-$550.**

Hamilton 748 men's wristwatch, **$50-$60.**

Hamilton electric wristwatch, **$125-$200.**

Hamilton 10 K.G.F. wristwatch, **$250-$350.**

Hamilton #987A 17J wristwatch, **$90-$110.**

Hamilton 982 wristwatch, **$60-$80.**

Hamilton LED wristwatch, **$50-$60.**

ILLINOIS WATCH CO.

Founded in 1869, this prolific Springfield, Ill., company turned out to be the third-largest producer behind Elgin and Waltham in terms of jeweled watches. In 1927, the company was sold to Hamilton. The line of wristwatches it produced is highly collectible. The company also made pocket watches, which were popular among railroad men; see Pages 72-80.

Illinois Grade 207 wristwatch, **$225-$300.**

Illinois Watch Co. circa 1920s, original band, **$175.**

Illinois Watch Co. sterling 15J, circa 1918, **$495-$795.**

Movement view of watch at left.

JAEGER-LECOULTRE

This fine company dates back to 1833, when Antoine LeCoultre established his watchmaking workshop in Le Sentier, Switzerland. In 1847, LeCoultre produced its first movement with a crown winding and setting system, eliminating the need for watch keys. In 1903, the company unveiled the world's flattest pocket watch caliber, and at 1.38 mm thick, it remains an unbroken record.

In 1925, tiny Art Deco watches were created, featuring the twin-level rectangular Duoplan movement, that were way ahead of their time in terms of accurate time-keeping. In 1929, LeCoultre reduced the mechanical watch movement to its smallest dimension ever—caliber 101. Measuring 14 x 4.8 x 3.4 mm, comprising 98 parts and weighing around one gram, it is still the world's smallest mechanical movement and is still in production.

In 1931, the company met the challenge to build a watch rugged enough to be worn in sporting events by inventing the Reverso. This wristwatch, with a swivel case, turns its back on shocks to protect the fragile glass. It is one of the few remaining authentic Art Deco creations still being produced. In 1953, Jaeger-LeCoultre developed the Futurematic. This watch is equipped with a power-reserve indicator and is the first automatic watch to require no winding crown. In 1956, the first automatic alarm wristwatch was created, the Memovox. The company still makes fabulous mechanical watches to this day in Le Sentier. It also made pocket watches; see P. 82.

LeCoultre Reverso, circa 1931, the legendary swivel watch, **$2,000-$9,000.**

LeCoultre Etrier models, circa 1930s, driver's style. Prices vary depending on SS or precious metals, **$300-$1,000.** *Photo courtesy of LeCoultre.*

LeCoultre Reverso, circa 1930s, 18k, **$7,000-$9,000.** *Photo courtesy of Antiquorum.*

Calendar watches. Top: Circa 1946, moon phases/calendar, **$2,000-$3,000**; bottom: Circa 1943, calendar/day/date, **$800-$1,200.** *Photo courtesy LeCoultre.*

LeCoultre Memovox, the first Le Coultre alarm wrist-watch manual wind, circa 1950. Price varies depending on SS, GF or precious metals, **$300-$900.** *Photo courtesy of LeCoultre.*

Jaeger-LeCoultre Mysterieuse, circa 1960s, 18k white, **$2,800-$3,500.** *Photo courtesy of Antiquorum.*

LeCoultre Master Mariner automatic, circa 1950s, power wind indicator, GF stainless back, **$195-$495.**

LeCoultre alarm, circa 1950s, raised numerals, stainless, **$295-$595.**

LeCoultre produces the smallest mechanical movement in the world, the Caliber 101. Circa 1929, Queen Elizabeth II wore this watch on the day of her coronation in 1952. This movement is still in production.

Jaeger-LeCoultre platinum, triple date moon phase, limited edition, **$11,000.**

LeCoultre ladies 14k gold, 1950s, **$350.**

Jaeger-LeCoultre "Reverso," dial reverses, 2002, **$2,400.**

LeCoultre automatic master mariner wristwatch, **$350-$450.**

LONGINES

Founded in 1867, Longines became the world's first watch trademark and the first Swiss company to assemble watches under one roof. In 1877, Longines won the first of its 10 World's Fair grand prizes and 28 gold medals, and it was the beginning of its rightful claim to the title of "The World's Most Honored Watch."

In 1899, the Duke of Abbruzi completed a successful Arctic Ocean expedition with Longines chronometers used as instrumentation. In 1927, Colonel Charles Lindbergh completed a first non-stop flight from New York to Paris using a Longines watch for time and instrumentation. See Pages 82-84.

From 1928 through 1938, the likes of Admiral Byrd, Amelia Earhart, Howard Hughes, Von Schiller, captain of the "Graf Zeppelin," and other adventurers placed their trust in Longines watches. In 1953, Longines developed the first quartz movement. Stainless steel automatics from the 1950s and 1960s are highly collectible, as are the early Longines wristwatches from the 1910s and 1920s.

Handmade 14k gold and rosewood watchband, with vintage 1955 Longines, **$1,500.** The rosewood band was made by the author.

Longines sterling with solid lugs, circa 1920s, enamel dial, **$150-$350.**

Longines ladies, circa mid-1920s, GF wire lugs, enamel bezel, 15J, **$125-$225.**

Longines enamel dial with Roman numerals, circa 1912, sterling wire lug case, 15J, **$195-$395.**

Longines 14k curved, circa 1940s, **$395-$695.**

Longines 17J GF, circa 1937, **$195-$295.**

Longines ladies, circa 1940s, 14k WG, fancy diamond case, **$495-$795.**

Longines 14k multicolored pink and green, circa 1940s, 17J faceted crystal, **$1,500-$2,000.**

Longines 17J, 14k, circa late 1940s early 1950s, flared case, **$395-$595.**

Longines 14k gold, manual wind, circa 1949, **$295-$595.**

Longines 14k white diamond dial, circa 1950, **$1,295-$1,695.**

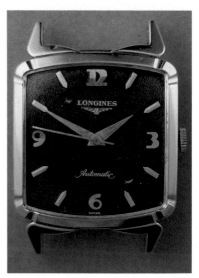

Longines 14k, circa 1950s, fancy lugs, faceted crystal, **$395-$695.**

Longines automatic, circa 1950s, 17J GF, original dial, **$195-$295.**

Longines with hour-glass case, circa 1950s, 17J GF, **$395-$595.**

Longines 14k with sub seconds, circa 1951, **$195-$495.**

Longines 17J, circa 1952, GF, **$100-$250.**

Longines Ultra Chron, circa 1960s, Auto/Date/ SS, **$295-$495.**

Longines 14k, circa 1960s, white sub seconds, **$195-$395.**

Longines 17 jewel #528, with eight diamonds, **$250-$300.**

Longines automatic with date, circa 1970s, stainless gray dial, **$295-$395.**

Longines-Wittnauer automatic wristwatch with box, **$400-$450.**

Longines ladies 14k white gold wristwatch, **$125-$175.**

Circa 1919 "Tonneau" style, enamel dial/Breguet style numerals, silver/935. *Photo courtesy Longines Museum Collection.*

Circa 1912 14k white gold case set with diamonds, 12 painted Breguet style numerals, external minute track. *Photo courtesy Longines Museum Collection.*

Circa 1937 bracelet band and case set with diamonds, silvered dial with Arabic numerals, square hour markers. *Photo courtesy Longines Museum Collection.*

Circa 1972 900/silver, ladies-men's wristwatches manual wind, the Serge Manzon Collection. *Photo courtesy Longines Museum Collection.*

MOVADO

In 1881, Achille Ditesheim, barely 19 years old and fresh out of watch-making school, founded his own watch-making company in Switzerland and was soon joined by three of his brothers.

In the first decade of the 20th century, when the market was still geared to pocket watches, Movado advanced the development of the wristwatch movement. The company was regarded as a pioneer in miniaturized movements and in 1912 introduced the Polyplan watch. An ultimate in conception, design, and engineering, Polyplan housed one of the earliest patented "form" movements, constructed on three planes inside a curved case that followed the natural contours of the wrist.

The 1930s were productive years for Movado. The factory developed its two-button Chronograph wristwatches with calendar indications that even included moon phases. Movado began production of wristwatches with automatic winding in 1945, and in 1946 it introduced the Calendomatic. These self-winding wristwatches of the 1940s are still among the most nostalgic collectibles ever produced by Movado. The next technological advancement in automatic watches came in 1956 with the introduction of the Kingmatic, a series of rotor-driven timepieces.

A prophetic moment for Movado occurred in 1947 when Nathan George Horwitt, an adherent of the Bauhaus design movement and one of America's outstanding designers, set out to simplify the wristwatch. His solution was to become a legend in modern design known as the Movado Museum Watch. "We do not know time as a number sequence," he said, "but by the position of the sun as the earth rotates." Applying this theory, he eliminated the numerals from the dial. Strongly influenced by the clean, spare lines of the Bauhaus, he designed a dial defined by a single gold dot symbolizing the sun at high noon, the hands suggesting the movement of the earth.

Horwitt's prototype was selected by the Museum of Modern Arts in 1959 for its permanent collection. The name, the Museum Watch, is so integral to the company's image that to many it is the first timepiece that comes to mind when they think of Movado. The company also made pocket watches; see Pages 85-87.

Movado Curviplan in 14k case, **$125-$175.**

Movado Zenith, **$30-$40.**

Movado Museum, circa 1976, 14k,
$2,000-$3,000.

Movado ladies, circa 1960s, 14k gold with
mesh band, extra small, **$695-$895.**

Movado, Tiffany & Co. Chronograph,
circa 1940s, 14k, **$1,500-$2,500.** *Photo
courtesy of Antiquorum.*

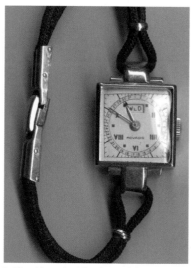

Ladies Movado 14k, day and date, 1940s,
$350.

OMEGA

This prolific Swiss company first started producing watches in 1848 and is famed for its timing of the Olympics for decades. In 1969, Neil Armstrong stepped onto the lunar surface wearing an Omega Speedmaster Professional, the only watch ever worn on the moon, and to this day the only watch issued to every NASA astronaut. Omega watches are very collectible, especially the "Seamaster" and the "Constellation" automatic models, as well as any of its Chronographs.

Some Omega pocket watches are on Pages 91-92.

Omega circa 1910, silver round wire lug, enamel dial, **$495-$695.**

Omega half hunter/demi-hunter, circa 1899, double-pointed hour hand-two dials, **$1,500-$2,500.** *Photo courtesy of Omega.*

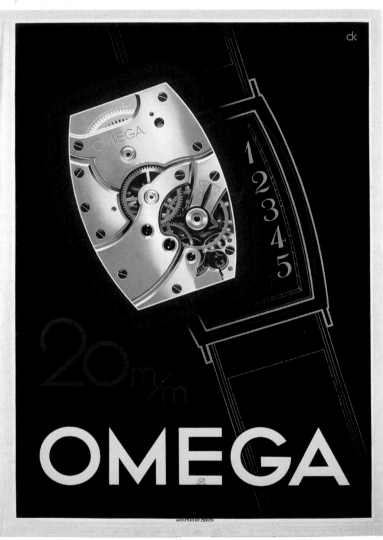

This Omega Art Deco ad dedicated the arrival of the caliber 20 that was launched in 1929.

Omega military, circa 1916, steel case with protective grill, caliber 13 movement, **$295-$595.** *Photo courtesy of Omega.*

Very rare Omega with minute repeater, circa 1892, no established value. *Photo courtesy of Omega.*

Omega 15J, manual wind, circa 1936, black dial Roman numerals, **$195-$395.**

Omega Chronometer, circa 1940s, pink gold, rare, **$900-$1,800.**

Omega military-RAF (Royal Air Force), circa 1950s, stainless, black dial, **$250-$750.**

Omega-Areo, oversized, 1950s airplane sub-seconds at 9, two-tone gold with black dial, base metal-pocket watch movement, **$250-$500.**

Omega 18J 14k, circa 1950, flared lugs, **$1,200-$1,500.**

Omega automatic, circa 1950s, stainless steel original mesh band, **$395-$695.**

Omega Ranchero, circa 1958, rare, stainless, ultra anti-magnetic, **$1,500-$2,500.**

Omega Speedmaster Professional, Chronograph, approved by NASA, stainless, **$900-$1,400.**

Omega Geneve, circa 1960s, automatic date, stainless, **$125-$275.**

Omega Speedmaster Professional, three-register Chronograph, circa 1966 (pre-moon), 17J stainless, **$1,000-$1,500.**

Omega bracelet watch, circa 1969, 14k with 14k bracelet, 17J, **$495-$795.**

Omega Constellation, Automatic Chronometer Date, circa 1970s, stainless, **$295-$495.**

Case back view of Observatory.

Omega Seamaster DeVille, circa 1973, stainless, SS Omega band, **$250-$500.**

A closeup view of the clasp and band.

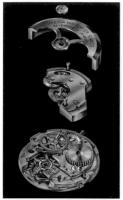

Omega early 1950 automatic-wind movement, caliber 455.

Omega 620 17 jewel, **$200-$250.**

Omega Automatic, **$90-$125.**

Omega Ladiematic, Swiss-made, **$125-$150.**

Omega 361 man's wristwatch, 17J, **$85-$95.**

Omega Automatic Seamaster, **$90-$125.**

It is not generally appreciated that in spite of Germany's occupation of every surrounding country, Switzerland did supply Great Britain with all the goods needed and ordered for the war effort. And we needed and ordered a lot.

To give only one instance: as every Airman knows, all the Navigational watches used by the R.A.F. during the war were made in Switzerland. Approximately half of these were

OMEGA
WATCHES
OMEGA WATCH CO. (ENGLAND) LTD.
26-30 HOLBORN VIADUCT, LONDON, E.C.1.
Makers of precision watches since 1848.

A British Omega watch ad featuring the caliber 30.

Printed in Switzerland

Supplément n° 2 / 1959

Various Omega wristwatch movements.

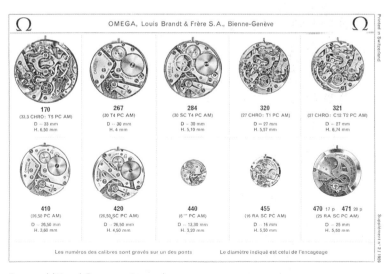

Printed in Switzerland

Supplément n° 2 / 1959

Some additional Omega wristwatch movements.

PATEK PHILIPPE

Founded in 1839 and considered to be one of the most important watchmakers in the world, this high-end company of Switzerland produced, and still creates, incredible works of the watch-making art. These watches are built to last and have been purchased throughout its 160-plus-year history by notables the likes of Queen Victoria, Kipling, Einstein, Tolstoy, and Marie Curie. Every Patek is collectible.

Some of the company's pocket watches are on Pages 93-96.

Patek Philippe rare model, circa 1950s, 18k rose gold with pink dial, sculptured lugs, indirect sweep seconds, **$9,000-$11,000.**

Movement view and inside case back of the watch above.

Patek Philippe Genève for Tiffany & Co., circa approximately 1964, 18k, 18J, **$3,000-$4,500.**

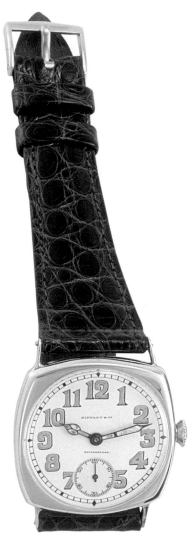

Patek Philippe made for Tiffany & Co., circa 1925, 18k cushion shape, **$9,000-$11,000.** *Photo courtesy of Antiquorum.*

Inside movement view of the watch at left.

Patek Philippe contract case 18k, converted pendant to wristwatch, dial refinished, **$2,500.**

Patek Philippe Calatrava (rare), original dial-manual wind, circa 1955, stainless-WP case, **$7,000-$12,000.**

Patek Philippe circa 1955, 18k yellow gold, **$4,200.**

Patek Philippe automatic with date, with gold rotor, 1950s, **$9,000.**

ROLEX

The Swiss company Rolex started producing the first truly waterproof watch, the "Rolex Oyster," in the later half of the 1920s. It has since been associated with high quality and durability. Watch connoisseurs love their Rolex, for they know that long after the price is forgotten, the quality remains.

Rolex ladies, circa 1922, 14k pink round diamond bezel, **$1,500-$2,000.**

Rolex Oyster, Chronometre Observatory, circa 1941, stainless steel, **$2,200-$2,600.**

Rolex Precision, circa 1940s, 18k with diamond-set bracelet, **$2,000-$3,000.** *Photo courtesy of Antiquorum.*

Rolex Oyster Royalite, circa 1942, stainless steel, **$1,250-$1,750**

Rolex Chronometer, circa 1944, 14k pink, **$1,500-$2,000.**

Rolex circa 1920s, mid-size sterling silver case, 15J, blue enamel bezel, **$1,500-$2,000.**

Rolex Viceroy, circa 1930s, stainless case with pink bezel, manual wind, **$1,200-$2,400.**

Rolex Oyster Bubble Back, circa 1940s, silver California dial, stainless steel, **$2,000-$4,000.**

Rolex Oyster Raleigh, Ref. #2784, circa 1940s, stainless steel, **$500-$700.**

Rolex Oyster, circa 1940s, stainless bubble back, refinished dial, **$900-$1,400.**

Rolex 14k pink stainless steel back, circa 1940s, 17J, hooded lugs, **$1,500-$2,000.**

Rolex ladies, circa 1940s to 1950s, 18k with 18k band, **$2,500-$3,500.**

Rolex Datejust, circa 1950, rare alternate red and black date, 18k pink gold case with black dial, **$3,500-$5,500.**

Rolex ladies, with diamonds, circa 1950, 14k white, **$2,000-$2,500.**

Rolex ref. #6234, Chronograph 72A, circa 1950s, rare, stainless steel original dial, **$11,000-$14,000.**

Rolex ref. #6234, Chronograph, circa 1950s, 14k gold case, luminous markers and hands, **$18,000-$20,000.**

Rolex 18k, circa late 1950s, Bombé lugs, **$2,500-$3,000.**

Rolex 14k, circa 1950s, **$2,200-$2,700.**

Rolex Datejust, circa 1953, 14k gold and stainless steel case, alternate red/black date, **$2,000-$2,500.**

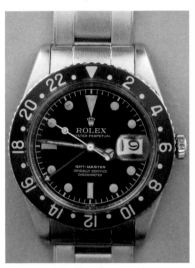

Rolex GMT Master ref #6542, circa 1955, blue and red bezel, stainless steel, **$2,500-$5,000.**

Rolex Tudor, Oyster Prince, circa late 1950s-1960s, self-winding, stainless steel, **$295-$495.**

Rolex Oyster Perpetual, stainless steel, circa 1958, **$1,400-$1,800.**

Rolex, Oyster Perpetual, circa 1959, two tone/ smooth bezel, **$1,500-$2,000.**

Rolex Oyster Perpetual, GMT Master, ref. #1675, circa 1968, stainless steel, **$2,000-$3,000.**

Rolex Queen Midas, circa 1960s, 18k midsize, **$3,500-$4,500.** *Photo courtesy of Antiquorum.*

Rolex Oyster Perpetual, ref. #5512, Submariner, circa 1960s, stainless steel, **$2,500-$3,500.**

Rolex circa late 1960s/early 1970s, diamond dial, stainless steel, **$1,200-$1,700.**

Rolex Datejust Ref 1625, circa late 1960s/
early 1970s, stainless steel, Thunderbird
bezel, **$2,500-$3,000.**

Rolex Oyster Precision, circa 1970,
stainless steel case with pink dial,
$1,000-$1,450.

Rolex Oyster Perpetual, Milgauss Chronometer, circa 1970s, stainless-ref. #1019,
ultra anti-magnetic, **$9,000-$12,000.**

Rolex Oyster Cosmograph, Daytona,
ref. #6263, circa 1970s, stainless steel,
$9,000-$12,000.

Rolex ref 6634, gold top over stainless backing, two-tone case, **$750-$1,050.**

Rolex Ladies Oyster Date, Ref. 6917, 18k, **$2,000-$3,000.**

Rolex ladies Perpetual, 18k, black dial sub seconds, **$1,500-$2,000.**

Rolex Oyster Date, stainless steel, **$900-$1,200.**

Rolex ladies, pink gold, 1940s, **$800.**

Rolex "Bubbleback" in stainless steel, 1940s, **$1,800.**

Rolex "Bubbleback" in pink gold, 1940s, **$7,500.**

Rolex Oyster Perpetual, yellow gold, circa 1960s, **$3,000.**

Rolex "Datejust," circa 1955, with early rivet band, **$1,400.**

Rolex "Tudor," 1960s, **$700.**

Rolex "Datejust," stainless steel and pink gold, 1972, **$2,200.**

Rolex Explorer II, circa 2002, **$3,500.**

Rolex Datejust, circa 1981, stainless steel, tapestry dial with jubilee band, **$1,700.**

Rolex Datejust, circa 1981, two-tone, jubilee band, **$2,500.**

Rolex diamond and 14k ladies wristwatch #1400, **$800-$1,000.**

Rolex Explorer, stainless steel, 1960s, **$6,000** with original box and papers; **$5,000** without.

Rolex GMT Master, stainless steel, late 1970s, **$3,500** with original box and papers; **$2,500** without.

Rolex Daytona, Model 6263, 18k, 1970s, **$45,000.**

Rolex, 14k, circa 1950, **$2,000.**

Rolex "Viceroy," pink gold and stainless steel, 1940s, **$2,000.**

SEIKO

This Japanese company was started in 1881 by Kintar Hattori and in 1892 began producing clocks. The first watches produced hit the market in 1924. The world's first production quartz watch was introduced by Seiko in 1969 and the company later introduced the first quartz chronograph.

Seiko is best known for its wristwatches and for its advanced technology, and makes both quartz and mechanical watches of varying prices. Its mechanical watches are the most prized by collectors.

Seiko 7J chrome, circa 1930s, Hermetic case within case, **$395-$595.**

Seiko automatic day date, circa 1970s, blue dial, stainless steel, **$75-$150.**

Seiko automatic day date, circa 1970s, two-tone dial, stainless steel, **$75-$150.**

Seiko Chronograph, automatic day date, circa 1970s, stainless steel, **$150-$300.**

Seiko World Time wristwatch, **$80-$100.**

Seiko Sportsmatic, water proof, **$20-$30.**

Seiko with wide band, 1970s, NOS, **$50.**

Seiko with wide band, 1970s, NOS, **$75.**

TISSOT

Charles F. Tissot founded a small watch factory in Le Locle, Switzerland in 1853. Tissot supplied watches to Russia and the "Tsar's Court." This fine company merged with the Omega Watch Co. in 1929 and still produces a line of quality watches today, including chronometer escapements.

Tissot Chronograph, circa late 1930s, stainless steel swivel lugs, **$1,300-$2,000.**

Tissot ladies, circa 1960s, gold top, plated stainless steel back, 17J, **$45-$95.**

VACHERON CONSTANTIN

One of the oldest Swiss watch companies, tracing back to the 1700s, it has created some of the most beautiful watches the world has ever seen.

Vacheron Constantin ranks among the top makers and is still in existence today. Its high-quality timepieces are extremely collectible and valuable.

Some of the companies pocket watches are on Pages 103-104.

Vacheron Constantin "Toledo," 18k white gold case and buckle, automatic, triple date moon phase, contemporary, **$15,000.**

Vacheron Constantin 18k pink, circa 1954, rare-style case, **$4,000-$6,000.** *Photo courtesy of Antiquorum.*

Vacheron Constantin automatic, circa 1966, 18k, **$2,000-$3,000.** *Photo courtesy of Antiquorum.*

WALTHAM WATCH CO. (AMERICAN WALTHAM WATCH CO.)

This is the granddaddy of large American watch companies. Its beginnings were in the early 1850s in Waltham, Mass., and it produced high-quality watches of every grade. Early examples of Waltham timepieces are valuable collectors' items and highly sought after.

This company was always innovative and the pioneering spirit of the people who worked at Waltham led to the development of the machinery that built the watch industry in this country.

Some of the companies pocket watches are on Pages 105-119.

Waltham base metal case with metal dial, circa 1910s, blue spade hands, 15J, **$95-$145.**

Waltham 15J with "sapphire" movement, circa 1930, ribbed case near lugs, yellowed crystal, **$50-$125.**

Waltham GF, circa 1915, wire lug enamel dial, rare offset face, **$700-$1,100.**

Waltham GF, circa 1934, 17J "Ruby" movement, **$100-$200.**

Inside view of the 17J "Ruby" movement.

Waltham 17J, circa 1934, engraved edge, white rolled gold plate, **$75-$150.**

Waltham Curvex style, GF, circa 1936, 17J 50mm lug to lug, **$295-$395.**

Waltham GF, circa 1937, 17J Crescent St. movement, **$100-$225.**

Waltham GF-black dial, circa 1950, 25J, **$100-$250.**

Waltham Premier, circa 1940s, RGP, 17J, **$45-$95.**

Waltham 21J, circa late 1950s/early 1960s, self-winding, stainless steel, **$95-$195.**

Waltham 17J, date, circa late 1950s/early 1960s, alarm, stainless steel, **$295-$495.**

Waltham Incabloc Swiss, circa late 1950s, GF 17J, sub-seconds, **$45-$95.**

Waltham ladies wristwatch, **$30-$40.**

Waltham quartz alarm chronograph, **$10-$15.**

Waltham 25 self-winding in Incabloc wrist-watch, **$60-$70.**

Waltham ruby 14k wristwatch, **$90-$110.**

MISCELLANEOUS WRISTWATCHES

Ball Trainmaster 25J wristwatch in 10k case, **$1,800-$2,200.**

Ball official RR standard trainmaster wristwatch, **$450-$550.**

Ball official RR standard wristwatch, **$200-$300.**

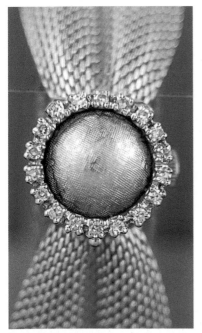

Baum & Mercier, bracelet with fliptop, circa 1950s, 14k, diamonds, .75ct. total wt., **$995-$1,495.**

Flip-top watch open.

Benny & Co. Chronograph, 2004, diamond bezel and dial, **$3,500.**

Bovet-Swiss chronograph, two register, circa 1940s, stainless steel case with square pushers, **$495-$895.**

Ernest Borel cocktail, circa 1960s, automatic, stainless steel, **$95-$195.**

Ernest Borel, circa 1950s, 18k square case, **$250-$500.**

Bucherer officially certified chronometer wristwatch, **$125-$150.**

Cartier France Art Deco purse attachment, exotic skin and tortoise shell, back wind and set, 18k, **$4,000-$6,000.**

Concord ladies retro watch, circa 1940s, platinum and diamond, rose gold, **$2,500-$3,500.**

Cartier "Roadster" ladies, stainless steel, 1990s, **$2,500.**

Concord 17J 14k Swiss ladies wristwatch, **$300-$350.**

Clinton 17 jewel wristwatch, **$15-$20.**

Corum peacock feather dial, circa 1970s, 18k tank style, **$800-$1,000.**

Swiss Croton, circa 1960s, sweep seconds, stainless steel, **$75-$175.**

Cyma Tavannes 7J movement, circa WW I, nickel case-grill guard, **$195-$395.**

Cyma sterling flip top push button, circa 1920s, radium enamel dial, **$495-$795.**

Cyma with top closed.

F. De Ferrari & Co., San Francisco, CA, circa 1920s, sterling enamel dial, Roman numerals, **$150-$350.**

Daniel Mink diver's watch, 2005, **$350.**

Douglas, 1970s, **$50.**

Dubey & Schaldenbrand, diamond bezel, 2004, **$4,200.**

Ebel ladies Swiss, circa 1960s, 14k with mesh band, **$425-$625.**

Ernest Morel wristwatch, **$175-$225.**

Eska mid-size early self winding, circa 1941, stainless steel, radium hands sweep second, **$150-$250.**

Gelbros Swiss, circa 1920s, fancy engraved chrome case, radium hands, **$100-$200.**

Restored Eterna, circa 1940s, two-tone stainless steel with gold lugs, **$195-$495.**

Favre Leuba, alarm, circa 1960s, seabird, stainless steel, **$250-$450.**

Geneve ladies, hooded lugs, pink gold, 1960s, **$250.**

Helbros 14k case, circa 1950s, diamond dial at 12, 3, and 9, 17J, **$125-$275.**

Refinished/restored Gueblin, circa 1940s, stainless steel, **$100-$300.**

Hansel Sloan and Co., Swiss, circa 1920s, silver/enamel dial, **$350-$500.**

High-grade Swiss movement of the Hansel watch above.

Heuer chronograph, 1972, **$1,500.**

Heuer Autavia, 1976, rare orange hands and markings, **$2,000.**

Hilton 17J-manual wind, circa 1950s, stainless steel, **$75-$150.**

Ingersoll Boy Scout wristwatch with leather band, **$90-$110.**

Ingersoll, circa 1920s, base metal, inexpensive early wristwatch, **$50-$100.**

Ingraham USA (2), circa 1940s, original crystal yellowed with age, 0 jewel, **$25-$75** each.

Jules Jurgenson Est 1740 Automatic, **$200-$275.**

Jacobs & Co. Chronograph, diamond bezel, 2004, **$3,200.**

Jacob & Co., five time zones, diamond bezel, circa 2004, **$3,200.**

Juvenia Swiss man's wristwatch 17J, **$40-$50.**

Wristwatches

Leora Swiss lapel watch, GP with enamel back, **$75-$175.**

Enamel case back of the watch at left.

Lionel collectible train wristwatch, **$15-$20.**

Marvin Watch Co.-Swiss, circa 1942, radium hands sub seconds, base metal, mirror effect on dial, **$50-$125.**

Mauran 15J 18k case ladies wristwatch, **$175-$200.**

Mido Multifort Grand Lux super automatic wristwatch, **$90-$125.**

Mondia Automatic wristwatch, **$30-$40.**

Mido multifort, circa 1950s, super automatic power wind, stainless, **$75-$175.**

Mido multifort automatic, circa 1940s, stainless steel, mid-size, **$75-$175.**

H.Y. Moser & Cie oversized conversion pocket watch to wristwatch, circa 1910s, **$295-$595.**

Franck Muller ladies, 18k white gold, 2005, **$6,000.**

Ulysse Nardin vintage wrist repeater, est. **$25,000-$40,000.**

New Haven Boy Scout wristwatch, **$90-$110.**

North Star, 1970s, **$50.**

Passeport Date wristwatch, **$70-$90.**

Pierre Cardin Australian opal wristwatch, **$175-$225.**

Pulsar alarm quartz wristwatch, **$20-$30.**

Pulsar quartz RR approved wristwatch, **$30-$40.**

Pulsar LED wristwatch, **$40-$50.**

Pulsar L.E.D. wristwatch, **$70-$90.**

Rulon, circa 1940s, .750 total weight diamonds, platinum, fancy bracelet band, **$900-$1,250.**

Shreve & Co., high grade Swiss movement, 18k, wire lug/enamel dial, **$600-$1,000.**

Movement view of the Shreve watch.

Swiss Tel Aviv 17J Israel wristwatch, **$10-$15.**

Swiss, circa 1910, silver wire lug, Roman numerals, **$95-$195.**

Ladies 14k wire lug, circa 1918, exploded numbers, **$125-$225.**

Swiss ladies pendant watch, enamel and gold case, **$150-$300.**

Swiss Civic, circa 1918, enamel dial wire lug, nickel, **$395-$695.**

Unknown maker, 1920s, ladies platinum with diamonds, **$500.**

Swiss Medana wire lug wristwatches, circa 1920s, **$50-$95** each.

Group of four Swiss la-
dies watches, wire lug,
$40-$95.

Group of six Swiss mid-
sized ladies watches,
circa 1910s-1920s, silver
wire lug enamel dials,
$75-$150 each.

Swiss pendant watch, circa 1920s, Art Deco, blue, purple, and green enamel, geometric design, **$95-$225.**

Back view of the Art Deco watch.

Swiss Ball pendant watch, round enameled, circa 1920s, turquoise enamel with gold accents, matching chain, **$95-$225.**

Pendant watch ornate top.

Pendant watch hanging.

Pendant watch, 14k, high-relief carved case with diamonds, high-grade Swiss movement, enamel dial, **$1,500-$2,500.**

Pendant watch back view.

Swiss Button Hole watch, gun metal and enamel with cylinder movement, **$95-$195.**

Swiss, circa 1910s, pin set onion crown, radium black dial, wire lug, **$600-$800.**

Button-hole watch, side view.

Swiss, circa 1910s, silver wire lug, radium dial and hands, **$150-$350.**

Swiss, circa 1920s, sterling case with wire lugs, **$250-$450.**

Swiss, pin set-wire lug, silver and gold engraved case back, enamel dial, **$295-$595.**

Swiss wire lug case back.

Swiss Time Square, circa 1930s, pin-back watch, sterling silver-Helbros movement, rubies-diamonds, **$250-$500.**

Swiss ladies, circa 1940, 14k rose gold case and band, copper dial, **$550-$950.**

Swiss Rima bracelet watch, circa 1940s, GF, 1-inch wide engraved band, **$95-$195.**

Tavannes, circa 1942, GF 17J, **$95-$195.**

Tiffany Swiss Pery 14k diamond ladies wristwatch, **$700-$900.**

Tiffany & Co. diamond wristwatch, **$2,500-$3,500.**

Universal Geneve wrist-
watch, **$2,200-$2,700.**

Vulcain Grand Prix wristwatch,
$90-$125.

Vulcain Swiss ladies
wristwatch, **$30-$40.**

Walkman Chronograph
wristwatch, **$200-$240.**

Wittnauer Geneve wristwatch, **$50-$60.**

Wittnauer electronic transistor-
ized wristwatch, **$40-$50.**

Wittnauer 2 Register Chronograph, circa
1950s, rare stainless steel, **$750.**

Zodiac automatic date wristwatch, **$50-$60.**

Cannon Paperweight with watch, Shet-
land, Germany, **$95-$195.**

Fancy enamel cherub and floral watch
stand, circa 1880, holds small ladies cylinder watch, **$700.**

Side view of the Cannon watch above.

Character Watches

This section contains a sampling of various character watches including cartoon characters, comic book heroes and timepieces featuring famous personalities, politicians and sports legends. If you are a fan of a specific character or personality, chances are you can find their face on a watch.

The following watches are listed alphabetically by character/person.

Exacta 1949 Babe Ruth wristwatch and baseball case, **$550-$650.**

U.S. Time 1950 Alice in Wonderland wristwatch, **$70-$90.**

U.S. Time 1948 Bambi #3842 wristwatch, **$40-$50.**

Swiss 1951 Bugs Bunny wristwatch, Rexall, with box, **$900-$1,100.**

Swiss 1964 Mattel Barbie wristwatch, **$30-$40.**

Betty Boop 1985 wristwatch S.F. CA, KFS, **$30-$40.**

Big Bad Wolf and the Three Little Pigs 1934 wristwatch, **$1,700-$2,000.**

Swiss 1951 Bugs Bunny wristwatch, **$50-$60.**

Fawcett 1948 Captain Marvel wristwatch, **$40-$50.**

Tom Corbett Space Cadet wristwatch, **$30-$40.**

U.S. Time 1948 Daisy Duck wristwatch, **$200-$250.**

Bradley 1958-62 Davy Crockett wristwatch, **$575-$625.**

Bradley Davy Crockett #LW-167 wristwatch, **$10-$15.**

New Haven 1935 Dick Tracy wristwatch, **$350-$400.**

New Haven 1948 Dick Tracy wristwatch, **$50-$60.**

New Haven 1948 Dick Tracy wristwatch, **$40-$50.**

New Haven 1951 Western Dick Tracy wristwatch, **$650-$750.**

Ingersoll 1935 Donald Duck wrist-watch with emblems, **$5,800-$6,200.**

U.S. Time 1955 Donald Duck wristwatch, **$70-$90.**

Donald Duck 1935 wristwatch with Mickey seconds disc, **$750-$850.**

Bradley Swiss Donald Duck wristwatch, HK strap, **$30-$40.**

Timex 1955 Donald Duck child's watch, **$30-$40.**

Ingersoll Donald Duck with Mickey wristwatch, **$400-$500.**

Bradley 50th Anniversary Donald Duck commemorative watch with packaging, **$20-$25.**

Gene Autry 1948 Champion wrist-watch, **$900-$1,100.**

Helbros 1971 Goofy running back-wards wristwatch, **$150-$200.**

U.S. Time 1950 Hopalong Cassidy in Box, NOS, **$150-$200.**

Fossil Gold Edition Goofy watch in origi-nal tin, **$65-$85.**

Gilbert 1965 James Bond Spy wristwatch, **$50-$60.**

New Haven 1951 Li'l Abner wristwatch, **$70-$90.**

New Haven 1948 Little Orphan Annie wristwatch, **$125-$175.**

New Haven USF 51 Li'l Abner Swiss wristwatch, **$40-$50.**

New Haven 1935 Little Orphan Annie sport wristwatch, **$400-$450.**

New Haven 1935 Harold Gray Little Orphan Annie watch, **$40-$50.**

Lone Ranger watch, **$70-$90.**

Fawcett 1948 Mary Marvel wristwatch, **$40-$50.**

Fawcett 1948 Mary Marvel Jr. wristwatch with box, **$90-$120.**

Mickey Mouse pocket watch and fob, **$200+**.

Ingersoll 1930s Mickey Mouse wristwatch, **$100-$140.**

Ingersoll 1933 Mickey Mouse wristwatch, **$90-$110.**

Ingersoll 1933 Mickey watch with original metal link band, **$130-$160.**

Ingersoll 1933 Mickey Mouse wristwatch, **$90-$125.**

Ingersoll 1933 Mickey Mouse wristwatch, leather band, **$100-$125.**

Ingersoll 1938 Mickey Mouse wristwatch, **$125-$175.**

Ingersoll 1934-37 Mickey Mouse wristwatch, **$160-$200.**

Ingersoll 1939 Mickey Mouse wristwatch, **$2,500-$3,000.**

Kelton U.S. Time 1946 Mickey Mouse wristwatch, **$350-$450.**

Ingersoll 1939 Mickey Mouse gold-tone model, **$900-$1,100.**

Ingersoll 1947 Mickey Mouse wristwatch, **$175-$200.**

Ingersoll 1947 Mickey Mouse wristwatch, **$200-$250.**

Ingersoll 1947 Mickey Mouse wristwatch, **$40-$50.**

U.S. Time 1948 #1842 Mickey Mouse wristwatch, **$30-$40.**

U.S. Time #1740 Mickey Mouse wristwatch, **$40-$50.**

U.S. Time 1949 Luminous Mickey wristwatch, **$50-$60.**

Ingersoll 1950s Mickey Mouse wristwatch, **$20-$25.**

Ingersoll 1950s Mickey Mouse wristwatch, **$10-$15.**

U.S. Time/Ingersoll 1955 Mickey Mouse, **$50-$60.**

U.S. Time/Ingersoll 1960s Mickey wristwatch, **$60-$70.**

Bradley 1973 Mickey Mouse wristwatch #6801, **$30-$40.**

Bradley 1973 Commemorative Mickey wristwatch, **$30-$40.**

Timex 1971 electric Mickey Mouse wristwatch, **$60-$70.**

Timex 1971 electric Mickey Mouse wristwatch, **$90-$110.**

Disneyland 1970s Mickey Mouse 17J wristwatch, **$30-$40.**

Bradley 1973 Mickey Mouse wristwatch, **$60-$70.**

Bradley 1970 Mickey Mouse wristwatch, **$20-$25.**

Bradley 1970s Mickey wristwatch, blister pack, **$10-$15.**

Bradley 1973 Time Mickey Mouse wristwatch, **$40-$50.**

Bradley Mickey Mouse Club wristwatch, **$30-$40.**

Bradley 1978 bobbing head Mickey wristwatch, **$30-$40.**

Ingersoll W.D. ENT. Mickey Mouse wristwatch, **$70-$90.**

Lorus Mickey Mouse quartz wristwatch, **$20-$25.**

Bradley 1975 Mickey wristwatch 7J Speidel, **$10-$15.**

Bradley 1976 Mickey Mouse digital wristwatch, **$30-$40.**

Bradley Swiss Minnie Mouse wristwatch, **$20-$25.**

Ingersoll Mickey Mouse wristwatch with emblems, **$175-$225.**

Timex electric W.D.P. Mickey Mouse wristwatch, **$20-$25.**

U.S. Time 1958 Minnie Mouse wristwatch with figure, **$100-$140.**

Bradley Time 1979 Mighty Mouse wristwatch, **$20-$25.**

Terry Toons Mighty Mouse Swiss wristwatch, **$20-$25.**

Bradley 1981 Swiss Mighty Mouse wristwatch, **$30-$40.**

American Time 1974 Richard Nixon "I'm Not a Crook" watch, **$20-$25.**

Bradley 1978 Oscar the Grouch wristwatch, new in box, **$30-$40.**

Swiss 1970 Planter's Peanuts calendar watch, **$30-$40.**

Playboy 1960s wristwatch, **$30-$40.**

Swiss Popeye K.F.S. wristwatch, **$30-$40.**

New Haven 1935 Popeye with Friends wristwatch, **$250-$350.**

Ingraham Porky Pig wristwatch, **$125-$150.**

New Haven 1949 Red Ryder wristwatch, **$400-$450.**

Ingraham 1954 Rockey Jones Space Ranger watch, **$80-$100.**

Ingraham 1951 Roy Rogers and Trigger wristwatch, **$70-$90.**

Ingraham 1951 Roy Rogers and Trigger wristwatch, **$80-$100.**

Bradley 1962 Dale Evans wristwatch with band, **$90-$110.**

Dale Evans and horse wristwatch with original band, **$50-$60.**

Rudolph the Rednose Reindeer watch, **$20+.**

Timex 1977 Schulz Tennis Snoopy wristwatch, **$10-$15.**

Timex 1969 Woodstock and Snoopy wristwatch, **$40-$50.**

Snow White and Dopey wristwatch with figure, **$60-$70.**

Ingersoll/US Time 1947 Snow White wristwatch, **$125-$150.**

Spiro Agnew watch and case, **$80-$90.**

Bradley 1980 Star Wars wristwatch, NIB/NOS, **$40-$50.**

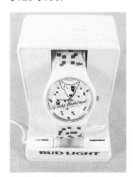

1986 Spuds MacKenzie Bud Light wristwatch, **$5-$10.**

Ingraham 1950 Woody Woodpecker wristwatch, **$125-$150.**

New Haven 1948 Superman wristwatch, **$250-$300.**

Resources

Dean Judy
P.O. Box 22676
Milwaukie, OR 97269
Web site: www.deanjudy.com

Cleves & Lonnemann Jewelers
319 Fairfield Ave.
Bellevue, KY 41073
859-261-3636

Tom Harris Auction Center
203 S. 18th Ave.
Marshalltown, IA 50158
641-754-4890
Web site: www.tomharrisauctions.com

Reyne Haines
www.reyne.com
513-504-8159
email: reynehaines@mindspring.com

Hake's Americana &
Collectibles Auctions
P.O. Box 1444
York, PA 17405
717-848-1333
www.hakes.com

Watch dealers
Eric Iskin
Olde Towne Jewelers
125 Fourth St.
Santa Rosa, CA 95401
707-577-8813
email: oldetown@sonic.net

Bill Hegner
116 Woodland Drive
Scotts Valley, CA
408-354-8366
email: ashwoof@cruzio.com

René Rondeau
Hamilton Electric Watch
P.O. Box 391
Corte Madera, CA 94976
415-924-6534
email: rene@hamiltonwristwatch.com
Web site: www.hamiltonwrist-watch.com

John Noveske
P.O. Box 789
Grants Pass, OR 97528
541-474-5547
email: John@watchbuyer.com
Web site: www.watchbuyer.com

Organizations
American Watchmakers-Clock-makers Institute
701 Enterprise Drive
Harrison, OH 45030-1696
Phone: 513-367-9800
Web site: www.awci.com

National Association of Watch
and Clock Collectors, Inc.
514 Poplar St.
Columbia, PA 17512
717-684-8261
Web site: www.nawcc.org

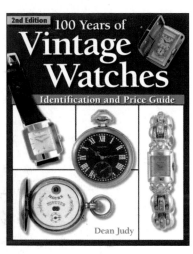
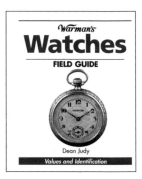